With the Guards Across the Pyrenees

With the Guards Across the Pyrenees

The Experiences of a British Officer of Wellington's Army During the Battles for the Fall of Napoleonic France, 1813

Robert Batty

With the Guards Across the Pyrenees: the Experiences of a British Officer of Wellington's Army During the Battles for the Fall of Napoleonic France, 1813
by Robert Batty

Published by Leonaur Ltd

Originally published in 1823 under the title:
Campaign of the Left Wing of the Allied Army in The Western Pyrenees and South of France, in the Years 1813-14; Under Field-Marshall the Marquess of Wellington

ISBN: 978-1-84677-288-7 (hardcover)
ISBN: 978-1-84677-287-0 (softcover)

http://www.leonaur.com

To

FIELD MARSHAL HIS GRACE
THE DUKE OF WELLINGTON, K.G.

This Narrative of the Operations of
the Left Wing of the Allied Army
in the Western Pyrenees
and South of France,
is Inscribed in Testimony of the
Highest Respect, Admiration
and Gratitude by
The Author

Contents

Preface

The difficulty of bringing together an accurate view of military operations, and more especially those which are carried on in a mountainous tract of country, where the several parts of an army are frequently separated and hidden from each other, makes it but the more desirable, and indeed essentially necessary for understanding the details of any combined movement, that Officers, in every corps of an army so circumstanced, should take down notes of such occurrences and manoeuvres as may fall under their immediate observation. We should then, by means of their united remarks, be enabled to arrive at a satisfactory explanation of the particular advantages of a successful plan of operations, and of the causes of failure in one that turned out to be otherwise. For, however well any proposed plan of a Campaign may be understood, the execution of it must always be liable to many variations, owing both to the nature of the country in which it is carried on, and to accidental circumstances which can neither be foreseen nor controlled.

With this object in view, the Author of the following Narrative determined, (partly from a conviction of their utility, and partly to gratify a beloved relative,) from the first moment of his joining the Left Wing of the Peninsular Army, as an Ensign in the Third Battalion of the First Foot

Guards, to make notes of every occurrence in the order in which they took place; and to employ all his leisure moments, which it will be seen could not have been many, in making military surveys trigonometrically of such portions of the country as were accessible; and also in taking sketches of the most remarkable scenery.

Owing to his arrival at a period of active operations, no opportunity occurred of forming associations with Officers in the Right Wing and Centre of the Army; and he has, for that reason, been compelled to limit his remarks almost wholly to the operations of the Left Wing. He feels, therefore, that much apology is necessary for presenting an imperfect Narrative to the Public, trusting, at the same time, that it may not be found wholly devoid of interest; neither will it prove altogether useless, if it should only be the means of stimulating others, whose abilities are more competent to the task, and whose opportunities of acquiring information were more ample than those of an Ensign doing regimental duty, to come forward with their share of observations; for unless such individual details be collected, the whole story of the Peninsular Campaign cannot be thoroughly understood, nor impartially related, by future historians. He is not sure, however, that his account of the Campaign of the Western Pyrenees would have met the public eye at this late period, had not present circumstances arisen, to throw an interest over that particular part of the Continent of which it treats; and did not a *possibility* exist of an eventual necessity, perhaps in no great length of time, for a British Army again to occupy its old positions, and to gain fresh laurels in the Mountain Passes of the Pyrenees.

Robert Batty

Chapter 1
After the Battle of Vitoria

It will not be necessary in order to elucidate the limited operations of one wing of the allied army, in the Western Pyrenees and South of France, that we should trace the whole progress of the war which led to the overthrow of the French dominion in the Peninsula; their connexion with prior events will be sufficiently understood, by briefly recurring to the principal movements which, subsequent to the battle of Vitoria, brought the allied forces to the Pyrenean frontier, where they occupied those positions which menaced the invasion of France.

The history of European warfare affords few examples of battles which have been more important in their results, or more brilliant in their achievement, than that of Vitoria. The campaign too which preceded it was distinguished by a series of the most able manoeuvres, compelling the enemy to retreat from the frontiers of Portugal to a defensive position behind the Ebro, without being able to oppose the allies in any general action. Thus, in the short space of one month, the influence which the French had held over the Peninsula, during several years, was brought to a fatal crisis. Indeed, so well aware was the intrusive King of the precarious state of his usurped throne, and of the hatred with which the French were regarded by the Spaniards; and so little did he calculate on the probability of his ever again being likely to return to the capital, that he had sent immense convoys, containing all the moveable plunder which, in the rapidity of his flight, could be scraped together, on the road to France; and having drawn up his army in front of Vitoria, he now endeavoured to protect, by a last effort, his broken power, and the safe convoy of his treasures out of Spain. The prominent features of the splendid victory gained by the allies on the memorable 21st of June are still fresh in recollection; the enemy being on that day driven from the field of action in the most complete disorder, with the loss of his artillery, treasure, baggage, convoys, and carriages; and compelled to seek safety in a rapid retreat by the road of Pamplona across the Pyrenees.

Lord Wellington, having thus completed the overthrow of the main body of the French forces, on the 21st of June, directed the left wing of the army, under Sir Thomas Graham, to advance on the following day upon Tolosa, with a view of intercepting the retreat of a French division, under General Foy, which then occupied Bilbao. The enemy, however, having ascertained the defeat of Joseph Buonaparte, immediately retreated, and, endeavoured to protect his retiring columns by barricading the approaches to Tolosa. Sir Thomas Graham attacked, and drove him from this post; and, on the 2d of July, the advanced guard pushed forward to the banks of the Bidassoa. Whilst these operations were carrying on upon the left flank, the third, fourth, seventh, and light divisions, supported by two brigades of cavalry, advanced upon Tudela; and the fifth and sixth divisions, supported by a brigade of cavalry, marched direct upon Logrono, with a view to cut off the retreat of two French divisions under General Clausel. This general, finding the direct road to France from Logrono occupied by the allies, countermarched upon Zaragossa, and gained the French frontier by the pass of Jaca.

Strong garrisons were left by the enemy in the fortresses of Pamplona and St. Sebastian. These places were immediately invested; and on the 30th of July, the garrison of Passages having surrendered, its port from this period became the *entrepôt* of supplies for the allied army; and its situation, so close to the line of operations, proved to be of the greatest utility in the succeeding campaign.

At the commencement of July, Marshal Soult, Duke of Dalmatia, being appointed to the chief command of the French forces, which were destined to act against Spain, with the title of Lieutenant of the Emperor, repaired without loss of time to the frontier, and commenced a thorough re-organization of the several corps of his army. The nomination of this Marshal to the command, from his known abilities, and from the high estimation in which he was held by the French soldiers of all ranks, was calculated to infuse new vigour into the disheartened and broken legions of Joseph's army. Great exertions were forthwith made for the re-equipment of the several corps. An abundant supply of every species of materiel was sent to replace the losses sustained; order was speedily restored; and the whole army distributed into four corps of infantry; consisting of the right, centre, left, and reserve, which were placed respectively under the orders of Generals Reille, Count d'Erlon, Clausel, and Villatte besides three divisions of cavalry, consisting of two of dragoons, and one of light horse, under the respective orders of Generals Treillard, Tilly, and Pierre Soult. These arrangements being completed, the Marshal collected supplies at St. Jean-Pied-de-Port, and without delay projected the relief of Pamplona, and the re-establishment of his army on the line of the Ebro.

In the meantime the Marquess of Wellington, on whom the Prince Regent had conferred the rank of Field Marshal, in reward for the late victory, concerted measures for the reduction of the fortresses still in possession of the enemy, and for the effectual exclusion of the French army from the Spanish territory. The want of an adequate siege train, and the distance from the source of supplies, prevented his undertaking the reduction of Pamplona by force; he, therefore, closely blockaded it with the Spanish corps under the Conde de Abisbal. Greater facilities of communication, however, enabled him to order the immediate, reduction of St. Sebastian, and its siege was commenced without delay.

To cover these operations, and to oppose the efforts which the enemy might make for the relief of these strong holds, the allied army was distributed in the following positions, for guarding the passes of the Pyrenees.

The right of the centre, commanded by Lieutenant-General Sir Rowland Hill, occupied the Valley of Bastan and, with Major-General Pringle's and Walker's brigades of the second division, under Lieutenant General the Hon. William Stewart, guarded the Passes of Maya. The minor passes of Col d'Ariette and Col d'Espegui, on the right, leading also into the Valley of Bastan, were held by Colonel Ashworth's and Brigadier-General Da Costa's Portuguese brigades, under the Conde de Amarante. Brigadier-General Campbell's Portuguese brigade of this division occupied a strong position on a mountain to the right of the village of Los Aldudes, and between the Valley of Aldudes and the Valley de Hayra; keeping communication with the Valley of Bastan on its left, through the Port de Berdaritz, and with the right wing of the army in the pass of Roncesvalles, through the Port d'Alalosti. The left of the centre consisted of the seventh division under Lieutenant-General the Earl of Dalhousie, and the light division under Major-General

Charles Baron Alten; the former was posted in the Pass of Etchalar; the latter on the mountain of Sta. Barbara and in the town of Bera. The sixth division under Major-General Pack occupied St. Estevan, and formed the reserve of the centre, ready to support the troops at Maya, or at Etchalar, as occasion might require.

The right wing of the army covered the direct approaches to Pamplona from St. Jean Pied-de-Port. Major-General Byng's brigade of the second division was in front, guarding the passes of Roncesvalles and Orbaicete; a division of Spanish infantry, under General Morillo, was in support at the latter post. The fourth division, commanded by Lieutenant-General the Hon. Sir Galbraith Lowry Cole, was in second line at Biscarret, in rear of the Pass of Roncesvalles. The third division, under Lieutenant-General Sir Thomas Picton, formed the reserve, and was stationed at Olaque.

The left wing, under Lieutenant-General Sir Thomas Graham, consisted of the first and fifth divisions, Major-General Lord Aylmer's brigade, and the fourth Spanish army, under Don Manuel Freyre, guarding the line of the Bidassoa from the Crown Mountain to the sea. The Spaniards, under Don Pedro Giron, with Brigadier-General Longa's division, kept up the communication with the left of the centre at Bera. The fifth division, under Major-General Oswald, consisting of the British brigades of Major-Generals Hay and Robinson, and of Major-General Spry's Portuguese brigade, was employed in carrying on the siege of St. Sebastian; whilst the first division, under Major-General Howard, consisting of the first and second brigades of Guards, under Colonel Maitland and Major-General Stopford, with the brigades of King's German Legion, and Lord Aylmer's brigade, were in position, covering the great road between Irun and Oyarzun, supporting the corps of Don Manuel Freyre, which crowned the heights of St. Marzial.

The contest at this period became more interesting than at any former time, from the opposition of two commanders of such high and distinguished reputation. Lord Wellington had hitherto overcome every French Marshal and General who had opposed him; and the result of the present campaign has proved how vainly the French looked for a more favourable issue under their new leader. We have already observed that the first object of the French Marshal was the relief of Pamplona. To effect this he placed his reserve under General Villatte, in the camp of Urogne, upon his right flank, to guard the line of the Bidassoa; whilst he withdrew his right wing to the neighbourhood of St. Jean Pied-de-Port; and there, uniting it with the left wing and a part of the centre, it formed the main body which Marshal Soult, on the morning of the 25th of July, conducted in person, to the attack of the right wing of the allies in the Pass of Roncesvalles. Count D'Erlon, with the two remaining divisions of the centre, was directed to make a simultaneous attack on the troops under Sir Rowland Hill, in the Passes of Maya. Both these attacks were, in the first instance, successful; the enemy overpowering, by superiority of numbers, the detached brigades which were guarding the Passes. Strong demonstrations were made against Major-General Byng's brigade, in advance of the right, whilst the main body of the enemy turned his flank by advancing along the lofty ridge of Arola, between the Vallée Carlos and the Vallée de Hayra. In the next place, by attacking and dislodging the Spaniards under Morillo, from the strong buildings in the ravine of Orbaicete on the extreme right, he was enabled boldly to push forward against the front of General Byng's brigade; and, although the fourth division, under General Cole, arrived in support, both were compelled to retire in the night to a position between Biscarret and Zubiri.

In the meantime Sir Rowland Hill, supported by Major-General Barnes's brigade, had been enabled to check the farther advance of the corps of Count D'Erlon; but the retrograde movement of the right wing led to the necessity of a corresponding one on his part. He, therefore, withdrew in the night to Elissondo, and from thence to a strong position at Irrueta, resting his left upon the Bidassoa. The Portuguese brigade, under Major-General Campbell, which had been stationed on the right of Los Aldudes, withdrew through the Pass of Renacabal, and joined the right wing in front of Zubiri.

Sir Thomas Picton moved up with the third division to support Sir Lowry Cole on the 26th, but the position being disadvantageous, and the French advancing with overwhelming numbers, made it expedient again to retreat. On the 27th, the retreat was continued, when the Marquess of Wellington, who had previously been superintending the movements of the left wing, fortunately arrived in time to direct the occupation of a position in front of the villages of Huarte and Villalba, and between the little rivers Arga and Lanz, so as to cover the roads leading from Elissondo and Roncesvalles to Pamplona; directing, at the same time, a portion of the Spaniards, under the Conde de Abisbal, to move up in support. This movement of the right wing obliged Sir Rowland Hill to remove on the 28th to a position at Lizasso.

The enemy had now approached to within a few miles of Pamplona; and, on the morning of the 28th, he commenced strenuous efforts to dislodge the allies from their position. Early on that morning, the 6th division, under Major-General Pack, fortunately arrived in support just prior to an attack which Marshal Soult directed from the right of his position in the valley of Lanz. The sixth division formed across the valley, and by its vigorous resistance, aided on its right flank by General Cole's division, wholly defeated the enemy's efforts to turn the left of the allies and penetrate by the valley. Failing on this point, the next attack was made against the centre, but all the efforts of the enemy, though often repeated against "the gallant fourth division," were repulsed by the steady conduct of the troops under Sir Lowry Cole. The arrival of the seventh division at Marcalain, between Sir Rowland Hill's position and the right wing, gave unity of action to the Allies, and assured the effectual obstruction of the enemy's further progress. Similar dispositions were made by Marshal Soult to connect his main body with the corps of Count d'Erlon, which had followed the march of General Hill, while moving a considerable force to his support in the valley of Lanz.

The Marquess of Wellington, foreseeing the enemy's intention, decided on attacking the troops in his immediate front between the Arga and Lanz, although the formidable position they occupied seemed almost impregnable. With this view, early on the morning of the 30th, he directed Sir Thomas Picton to move by the valley of Arga upon the French left, whilst Lord Dalhousie, by turning their right in the valley of Lanz, should endanger the safety of the centre on the crest of the position. General Pakenham, after General Pack was wounded, led the sixth division against Saurauren; whilst Sir Lowry Cole, with the fourth division, attacked in front, briskly following up the enemy as he wavered and retired from the position. Count d'Erlon had meanwhile been manoeuvring against the left of Sir Rowland Hill; but the latter, having taken up more favourable ground close in rear, with his left thrown back, bade defiance to every further effort against him. Marshal Wellington having now, in his turn, become the assailant, successively dislodged the enemy from every position where an attempt was made to withstand his progress; pressing close on the

French columns through the valley of Bastan, many prisoners were taken; and keeping up an unrelaxed pursuit on the 31st, the Allies were again masters of the passes through the mountains, and occupied nearly the same positions as before the attack of the 25th.

During these operations, the siege of St. Sebastian was converted into a strict blockade; but, on their successful termination, and the arrival of reinforcements and fresh supplies from England, it was resolved to renew it with increased vigour. The land forces now engaged in the siege were greatly aided by a squadron under the orders of Sir George Collier. A number of guns from the ships, with gunners to work them, were landed and formed into a battery, which contributed much to the success of the besiegers. On every occasion the zeal of the soldiers, and the ability of the engineers, were nobly displayed. Eighty pieces of cannon, under the chief direction of Lieutenant-Colonel Dickson, were now employed against the walls of the fortress. The earth shook with the tremendous concussion of this prodigious cannonade. On the 31st of August the troops moved to the assault; the defenders, under General Hey, showed a worthy constancy; repeatedly driving down the assailants from the crest of the breach, they as often returned, till the artillery were at length compelled to direct their fire against the enemy, immediately over the heads of those destined for the assault; and this bold measure fortunately succeeded in shaking the firmness of the defenders. In a fresh assault the troops gained possession of the summit, and in a short time of the whole town, taking nearly seven hundred prisoners.

On the same day Marshal Soult directed an attack to be made on the left wing of the Allies covering the siege; his principal efforts were directed against the corps of Don Manuel Freyre, strongly posted on the heights of St. Marzial, and extending their right in advance of the Crown Mountain, in order to cover the different fords across the Bidassoa, in front of their position. The seventh and first divisions were placed respectively in support of the right and left flank of the Spaniards.

The French columns daringly crossed the river by fords opposite to the strongest points of the allied position, and made several strenuous efforts to dislodge the Spaniards; but the latter, with the greatest gallantry, constantly drove the enemy down, causing him severe losses at every renewed trial. Whilst the action was going on at this part, strong columns of the enemy forded the Bidassoa, in the neighbourhood of Bera and Salines; but the Marquess of Wellington, penetrating the intention of the enemy to turn the flank of his left wing, by an advance upon the Crown Mountain and Oyarzun, ordered the seventh division up to support the advanced posts. The enemy was by this means checked, and, at night compelled to withdraw again behind the Bidassoa. The manoeuvre of sending a force by the valley of Cinco Villas upon the Crown Mountain and Oyarzun has been repeatedly practised by French commanders, in former wars, upon this point; and was successfully executed by Bonnivet in 1521, by Berwick in 1718, and again by the divisions of Moncey and Delaborde in the revolutionary war of 1794. The brunt of the action on the right was on this occasion sustained by Major-General Inglis's brigade of the seventh division; but upon the left the contest was wholly supported by the Spaniards, who at night re-established their sentinels on the banks of the Bidassoa.

In this manner every attempt made by the enemy for the relief of the fortresses of Pamplona and St. Sebastian was completely defeated. There now only remained the Castle of La Motte, situated on the high rock of St. Sebastian, to be gained by the Allies, for the entire liberation of the left wing to prosecute its further operations. This was speedily accomplished; for batteries were opened against the Castle on the morning of the 8th of September with such terrific effect, that the governor, General Rey, with the remainder of his garrison, amounting in men and officers to upwards of one thousand eight hundred, capitulated in the afternoon, and were made prisoners of war.

CHAPTER 2

Crossing the Bidassoa

Immediately after the fall of St. Sebastian, and indeed previous to its siege, the army had every reason to believe that the Marquess of Wellington had determined on the invasion of France. This opinion in the allied troops was strengthened by the appearance of Rear Admiral Martin at head-quarters, then at Lezaca, about the 21st of September; the object of whose mission was understood to be that of arranging the necessary naval assistance and co-operation in this important undertaking. This co-operation of a naval force was deemed of such essential use, and the value of it so duly appreciated by the Field Marshal, that he has often been heard to say, "It is our maritime superiority that enables me to maintain my army, where that of the enemy would have perished." Indeed the almost daily supplies and reinforcements sent out from England to the north coast of Spain, in transports convoyed by ships of war, alone enabled the army in this exhausted country, to carry on its operations in that part of it. During the month of August, upwards of twenty sail of ships of war with their convoys arrived in, and before, the harbour of Passages, which was the principal port of communication with head-quarters.

Independent of the ships of war upon this coast in communication with the army, amounting of all classes to about twenty sail, two line of battle ships, of the squadron blockading Rochfort, were considered as disposable for any service that the Marquess might require, and which they might undertake with safety, on so dangerous a coast as that between Bayonne and Passages. One of these ships was directed to show herself occasionally from the Cordouan light-house to Arcassons.

This force was chiefly employed in blockading St. Sebastian's, Santona, the mouth of the Bidassoa, and the Adour; as well as in intercepting the enemy's communications by sea, particularly with St. Jean de Luz. We have already seen the great assistance rendered to the army in the reduction of St. Sebastian, by the squadron under Sir George Collier, both by the ships blockading the harbour, and by the exertions of the gallant seamen in the batteries commanded by Lieutenant O'Reilly.

The future progress of the army was equally assisted by this squadron, which hovered along the coast, supporting, like a moveable fortress, the left wing, as it took up its various positions. At this time the mouth of the Bidassoa was guarded by His Majesty's ship Constant, commanded by Lieutenant Stokes, and the sailors had possession of Figueras Castle, which was only distant from the French guardhouse about three thousand yards. The anchorage ground off this river is good but in the winter months the sea generally runs so high, that no vessel, belonging to the country, ever attempts to ride in the bay; during these months no fishing boats venture to cross the bar which, at low spring tides, has only a depth of four feet water; but these tides rise sixteen feet. The whole extent of the anchoring ground in the bay was within cannon-shot of the French batteries. While the navy was thus employed upon this dangerous coast, the army was rapidly repairing its losses, and refitting in every article requisite for a renewal of active operations.

On the 31st of September, fifteen sail of transports entered the harbour of Passages with a reinforcement of seven hundred men of the foot guards. On the following day these troops landed, and marched up to the camp of the first division in rear of Irun.

Nothing can be more striking than the entrance of the harbour of Passages, as seen from the Bay of Biscay. On approaching this part of the Spanish coast, no indication of a navigable inlet is at first view discernible. On closer examination, however, we discover a deep narrow cleft in the precipitous range of rocky mountains which bound the coast, and rise abruptly from it; and it is only on the vessel's approach immediately beneath the rugged steep, that those on board perceive the narrow channel between two lofty walls of solid rock. The salient angles jutting from each side of this channel still screen from view the little town of the same name, and the vessels, in the harbour close to it. Having cleared this narrow and gloomy canal, a sudden and surprising change takes place; the town or rather village of Passages is discovered skirting the little harbour, the mountains almost hanging over the houses. Many of the dwellings are half formed by excavations from the rock, their fronts only being walled up. The width between the rocks and the water is in most places only just sufficient for a cart-road, and the houses in some places are built over this road, leaving only an archway for passengers. A little higher up, the harbour widens, and the open country begins to be discovered, bounded however by a succession of lofty ridges of mountain, which are themselves surmounted by the huge and rugged masses of the great Pyrenean chain.

A small open space on the margin of the harbour is dignified with the name of the square, or market-place. At the time of which we are speaking, this spot was the scene of the greatest bustle; for it was here that the troops sent from England were continually landing, together with ammunition, provisions, and stores of various kinds, for the use of the army. The horses for the cavalry were lowered from the transports into the water, and, guided by a rope, swam to the shore. The sudden transition from the intense heat in the holds of the transports to the cold temperature of the sea was the cause of death to several of these animals.

Passages was, besides, the resort of officers and soldiers, both English, Spanish, and Portuguese, for the purchase of provisions, or articles of equipment, imported from England by the sutlers, saddlers, and other followers of the camp. The motley peasantry from the surrounding mountains brought their vegetables to market here, and the whole formed a scene of indescribable bustle and noise, of endless variety of costume and confusion of languages.

The coast from Passages to the mouth of the Bidassoa is formed by the steep rocky side of the mountain of Jaysquibel, terminating at the mouth of the Bidassoa in a rocky promontory, called the Point of Figueras. Its crest is narrow and difficult of access, and the highest point elevated one thousand seven hundred feet nearly above the level of the sea. This mountain is separated from the chain of the Pyrenees by a broad valley of irregular features, intersected by a succession of hills and dales, and abounding in clumps of wood; here and there may be seen a little hamlet, and the smiling cottages of the peasantry lie scattered over the surface of the valley. The whitened walls, the projecting roofs, and the gables and wooden balconies of these cottages, amidst the deep gloom of the surrounding mountains, give to the scene a lively and a most picturesque effect. The little towns of Ernani and Oyarzun, and the village of Lesso, are situated in this valley, through which also the great road, leading from Vitoria to Irun, passes. The ground is only partially cultivated, and the chief produce seemed to be Indian corn or maize.

From the heights above Irun the view of the surrounding scenery is extremely fine; the Bidassoa is seen spreading out into a broad river, and flowing into the Bay of Biscay, between the mountain of Jaysquibel on the left hand, and the heights on the French side on the right. At the foot of the mountain, on the left, stands the celebrated town, or city, of Fontarabia, or Fuentarabia, (Fons Rapidus,) close to the margin of the river: opposite to it, on the French side, is the little town of Hendaye, or Andaye, famed for the excellence of its brandy. The town of Irun stands near the banks of the river, about a mile from the site of the bridge, which connects the great road leading from Vitoria to St. Jean de Luz and Bayonne. The bridge had been destroyed by the French, on their retreat within their own frontier before the troops under Sir Thomas Graham and the houses adjoining to it were loop-holed, and converted into a strong defensive post, which was now occupied by a piquet, with a line of sentinels stationed along the banks of the river, and in the Isle de la Conférence, just below the spot.

The Isle de la Conférence, (or, as it is called, the Isle of Pheasants) received its name from the celebrated treaty between France and Spain, which was ratified on this island, when Louis XIV. was betrothed to Maria Theresa of Austria, only daughter of Philip IV. of Spain, on the 3d of June, 1660. On the other side of Irun the mountains rise in a succession of steep acclivities, towering one above another till the whole are surmounted by the rugged points of the Crown Mountain, or Monte de Haya. The slopes of this chain are connected by a narrow ridge with the Heights of St. Marzial, so named from a chapel dedicated to that saint, which stands on a pointed rock at the western extremity.

The view of the amphitheatre of mountains from the rock of St. Marzial is remarkably grand, the sides of the mountain being worn into deep glens by the torrents which fall in the rainy season; and these glens are richly wooded with oak and chestnut. The annexed view is from the rocky point of St. Marzial; it exhibits the range of mountains occupied by Lord Aylmer's British Brigade, and the first division, under Major-General Howard, supporting the Spaniards of Don M. Freyre, who were encamped on the Heights of St. Marzial, guarding with their sentinels the line of the Bidassoa. A line of entrenchments and redoubts was formed from the Crown Mountain to the Point of Figueras. They were eight in number, the first nearest to the Crown Mountain, and the last about half a mile beyond Fontarabia. The fifth, a very strong redoubt, was constructed close to the town of Irun, and was intended to cover the approach to it by the great road from France. Working parties were constantly employed on these defences until the recommencement of active operations. The troops, which, in the annexed view, are seen ascending the heights, indicate the roads by which the Portuguese brigade of Brigadier-General Wilson, and the first brigade of Guards under Colonel Maitland, advanced across the Height of St. Marzial to the fords by which they crossed the Bidassoa, in the subsequent attack of the 7th of October.

From every eminence the romantic aspect of the surrounding country presents itself in new and varied forms of grandeur and beauty. The buildings, though thinly scattered over the country, are picturesque, and, like most of the Spanish houses, have large projecting roofs. Glazed windows are rarely seen, shutters being almost every where the substitute. There are but few vineyards in this vicinity, excepting on the slopes of Jaysquibel near Fontarabia; but about the houses, the vine is every where reared. The inhabitants are a strong and well-proportioned race, having jet black hair, black eyes, and deep brown complexions. The women, many of them tall and with handsome features, wear their hair in a huge plait, which hangs down the back below the waist; but neither sex were observed to have those "ears of uncommon size," which Buffon says Nature has given to the inhabitants of the banks of the Bidassoa.

The climate appears to be very variable, as is usual in the neighbourhood of a range of lofty mountains. The thermometer, early in the morning, was frequently up at 70°, and rose gradually till the latter part of the day; and on the next day, at the same hour, it was as frequently at, or even below, 60°. The evenings generally were remarkably beautiful; the splendid colouring of the immense amphitheatre of mountains, in the glowing rays of sunset, is beyond description.

The leisure afforded, whilst the preparations we have described were going forward, gave the officers an opportunity of making excursions, and examining the most interesting scenes in the neighbourhood; but the possibility of being at any moment ordered to advance against the enemy, prevented these rambles being of any very great extent; several, however, ventured across the mountains, to visit their friends or relations in other regiments, and to ascertain which of them still survived; for, in so great an extent of country as the army now occupied, and especially in one so divided by ranges of lofty mountains, the events which took place, even in contiguous divisions of the army, were scarcely known to each other, until the arrival of Gazettes from England brought the details of the various operations, with lists of the killed and wounded.

Amidst the interesting objects that surrounded us, the town of Fontarabia claimed a due share of attention, though the ruinous heaps of its fortifications, which were blown up in the war of the Revolution, gave it a desolate and cheerless aspect. It stands on a small peninsular eminence, contiguous to the Bidassoa, which, at high water, washes the ruins of its walls; but which, when the tide is out, leaves a considerable extent of sand on both sides of the channel. It is, in fact, what is usually called a dry harbour. The annexed view is taken from the sands, and shows the broken remains of the fortifications. The streets are remarkably narrow, the houses have large projecting roofs, and exhibit all the characteristics of a Spanish town; most of the windows have large balconies in front. The view down the main street looks directly towards the rugged summit of Monte de Haya, or the Crown Mountain. Nothing could be more desolate than the appearance of the town at this period; all the houses were shut up, and scarcely a single inhabitant showed himself out of doors. At a little distance below the town, and on the banks of the river, is a large suburb, called the Suburb of the Magdalen, composed in great part of fishermen's houses, delightfully situated close to the water's edge.

A staff-officer was at this time employed in ascertaining the situation of the fords, by which columns of infantry might pass the river near its mouth. With this view, and to avoid exciting suspicion, some of the Spanish fishermen were prevailed on to undertake to wade through the channel at low water; and, under the appearance of being occupied in their usual employment of fishing, they proceeded a considerable distance into the river; but being apprehensive of being taken by the French sentries, who were guarding the right bank, they at first returned without ascertaining the practicability of fording it. Threats, however, at length, induced one man to go fairly through; and as there was a considerable extent of sand between the channel and the right bank, he had time to return in safety, apparently without having excited the least suspicion in the enemy. Similar experiments being afterwards made on different points, three fords were discovered, which were considered available, between the island of the Conférence and the mouth of the river.

Until the surrender of Pamplona it was not possible to act on the offensive upon a great scale; but in the meantime the Marquess of Wellington resolved to cross the Bidassoa, with the left wing of his army, and to occupy with it a range of heights, on the right bank of the river, from the Great Mountain of La Rhune to the sea. Rumours of the intended movement reached the camp on the evening of the 6th of October. The day had been intensely hot, and in the evening heavy masses of clouds gathered over the mountains, casting a deep gloom over the whole country, and at length burst in a violent thunder-storm, accompanied with rain and hail. Towards the morning the storm passed over to the French side of the river; and, we were willing to think, prevented the enemy's sentries from hearing the noise of our artillery, pontoon wagons, caissons, and other carriages, advancing to take their several stations preparatory to the intended attack.

The dispositions for attack were as follow: — On the extreme left the fifth division, Lord Aylmer's Brigade, and Major-General Spry's Portuguese Brigade, were to cross by the three fords between the Isle de la Conférence and the mouth of the river. One of these brigades was concealed till the moment of attack in the ditch behind the town of Fontarabia; the other two behind large embankments, enclosing meadows between Irun and Fontarabia, immediately in front of the Capuchin Convent. On the right of the fifth division were the first division and Brigadier-General Wilson's Portuguese Brigade, concealed behind some small eminences at the foot of the heights of St. Marzial. These were to cross by fords at the site of the old bridge of Irun, and higher up the river, opposite the centre of St. Marzial height. The second brigade of Guards under Major-General Stopford, with the brigades of the King's German Legion, below the old bridge, and the first brigade of Guards under Colonel Maitland, preceded by Wilson's Portuguese, at the ford higher up. To the right of these the fourth Spanish army, under General Freyre, was to cross at fords in front of Buriatou, and the mountain of Mandalle, in three columns, and by gaining the summits of the mountains, to turn the flank of the enemy in his camp in front of Urogne. The light division, under General Alten, was to attack the enemy posted on the mountain of Commissari, and in the Pass of Bera; whilst Don Pedro Giron, on the extreme right, attacked the position of Great La Rhune.

At three o'clock in the morning of the 7th of October, the troops were under arms. The first division moved down from its camp into the great road leading to Irun. The tents were left standing, that the enemy, as dawn appeared, might not discover any sign of the intended movement. Every preparation was made as silently as possible, but still the noise of the artillery and pontoon train, moving slowly forward on the great road, might be distinctly heard. The inhabitants of Irun were all gazing out of their windows as the troops filed through the town; vivid flashes of lightning glared occasionally, but the body of the storm of the preceding evening, had passed over to the French side of the river. Under all these circumstances, the troops fortunately arrived at their appointed stations without having been noticed by the enemy.

Owing to the considerable bend of the river below the bridge of Irun, it was necessary that the fifth division should be the first to cross, and as soon as it should be sufficiently advanced, the other columns of the first division were directed to cross, and the whole corps to advance up the heights together. At a few minutes past seven o'clock, it being then low water, the columns near Fontarabia were discerned crossing the sands and entering the river, which they forded, and the whole of the three columns advanced steadily but slowly, preceded by the light companies of their respective brigades. The annexed view will show the extent of the Bidassoa at high water, between Andaye and Fontarabia; and, as the tide rises sixteen feet, it may be easily imagined that a good deal of anxiety prevailed to seize the most favourable moment for fording, the more so, as any untoward circumstance, creating even a short delay, might occasion the most serious consequences.

To ensure the support and co-operation of the other columns, a rocket was fired from the steeple at Fontarabia, as the signal for their simultaneous advance; and such had been the caution observed in every preparatory step, that the enemy did not commence firing till the heads of the columns were nearly half over. The upper column, owing to a mistake in entering the ford at a wrong point, got into very deep water, and was obliged to turn lower down where the channel is divided by a sand-bank; it then advanced again, and got safe over. The fifth division had no sooner gained the right bank, than the enemy's picquets commenced a brisk fire from behind every hedge, ditch, and wall, and from the windows of the houses around Andaye. The light troops rapidly drove the enemy from these defences, and the columns continued their advance in excellent order, and began to take up their proper distances preparatory to attacking the French line, which was now forming on the nearest range of hills. The first division was then ordered to cross, to support the right flank of the fifth division. Some artillery were brought to an entrenchment, which had been purposely thrown up opposite to the old bridge, and by a brisk fire, aided by the light infantry, soon dislodged the French piquet from the loop-holed houses guarding the pass. The second brigade of Guards and the King's German Legion crossed immediately after, and covered the formation of a pontoon bridge, which was rapidly laid down for the passage of the artillery a little way higher up the river. The Portuguese under Brigadier-General Wilson, followed by the first brigade of Guards under Colonel Maitland, in the mean time crossed over the heights of St. Marzial, and forded the river directly in front. Cannon and howitzers were planted on the top of St. Marzial, and by their fire covered the passage of the troops; the howitzers were of essential service in clearing away the enemy's picquets from the bank of the river.

The view of the action from the summit of St. Marzial was most magnificent, as it commanded a prospect of the whole range of the enemy's position from the mountain of Mandalle to the sea. Lord Wellington took his station at this point, and appeared in the highest spirits, at the successful progress of his troops. The French artillery commenced firing from the summit of their position upon the several columns as they advanced, and their infantry formed their line upon the height to await the approach of the assailants. By this time the Spaniards, under Don Manuel Freyre, had succeeded in crossing by the upper fords, and after bravely compelling the enemy's picquets to retreat from their entrenchments on the slopes of the mountains, were now rapidly gaining the summit of Mandalle, notwithstanding the strong position held by the French. About a mile above the point where the first brigade of Guards, and Wilson's Portuguese, forded the river, is the hamlet of Buriatou. In rear of it the French had a large hutted camp, and some obstinate skirmishing took place between them and the Spaniards, till the latter having turned their flank, the enemy retreated.

The severest part of the contest on the left was maintained by the fifth division. Major-General Hay's brigade, consisting of the first, ninth, and thirty-eighth regiments, had to attack the enemy in three successive positions, which he took up each time in good order, but the brave fifth division charged and dislodged him in succession from each of these posts. In the last, the enemy found his right flank turned by the brigade which had crossed below Fontarabia, and which, by following the line of coast for some distance, and then taking an oblique direction to its right, came almost unperceived in rear of the enemy's right wing, and thus compelled him to seek safety in a rapid retreat by the great road through Urogne. The lines which formed to oppose Colonel Maitland's brigade and the Portuguese, seeing both flanks turned, (their left by the Spaniards, and their right by the fifth division,) did not await a close approach, and on gaining the crest of the position, three pieces of cannon, unspiked, were found in one of the entrenchments.

The attack made by the light division had been equally successful. The French at this part were strongly entrenched on the summits and slopes of the steep mountains immediately above the town of Bera, and their hutted camps were fortified upon every accessible side. The enemy attempted to withstand the advance of Major-General Skerret's brigade, led by Colonel Colborne, but he was driven from all the entrenchments of this side by the brave and undaunted advance of the fifty-second, and the second battalion of the ninety-fifth, supported by the brigade of Portuguese Caçadores, attached to the light division. As the ascent to this fortified camp was by a narrow zigzag path up a very steep rocky mountain, defended at every eminence by entrenchments, the attack of it was one of great hazard, and it required the promptest and boldest exertions of the troops to overcome the obstacles opposed to them. This was done by repeated charges with the bayonet. The loss in Colonel Colborne's brigade and the Portuguese Caçadores was consequently severe.

The position of Mont de Commissari is one of those occupied during the war of the revolution in 1793. A line drawn from the point of Great La Rhune, through the camp on Mount Commissari, to the Bidassoa below Salines, marks the frontiers of France and Spain. The capture of these entrenchments, therefore, placed the light division also upon the French territory.

The Pass of Bera, close upon the right of this mountain, was carried by the brigade under Major-General Kempt, consisting of the forty-third, and first and third battalions of the ninety-fifth. Every where the troops were successful, with the single exception, towards the evening, of the Spaniards under General Giron, who were attempting to gain possession of the summit of Great La Rhune. The firing in all other parts had ceased early in the afternoon, but was kept up till quite dark in the attack of La Rhune. The outline of this mountain, seen from the camp near Urogne, is that of a high cone; and at night, during the firing, it exhibited the beautiful appearance of being illuminated. On the summit stands the ruins of a little chapel, which the French had converted into a military post. The rock on which it was built appeared to be inaccessible, and it was in the attempts made to storm it that the firing was kept up during the night. On the following morning the Spaniards succeeded in gaining possession of this post; and thus the whole army was established in positions commanding views of the plains of France to an amazing extent.

Mount La Rhune was obstinately contested by the two nations in the revolutionary war; and it was now a subject of congratulation, as well as surprise, to all the officers of the army, that this formidable position of the enemy had been gained with such comparatively small loss to the Allies: the total loss of British, Portuguese, and Spanish, both in the attack upon the left and in the Pass of Bera, amounting, in killed, wounded, and missing, to no more than one thousand five hundred and sixty, including officers. It was owing, in all probability, in the first place, to the secrecy with which the attack was planned and commenced; and, in the next, to the apparent confidence of the enemy, that at this late period of the year, the Allies would rest satisfied with having liberated the Spanish territory, and established their army in positions the most favourable for its defence. The garrison of Pamplona likewise, not having yet surrendered, might have induced the French to suppose that, at all events, Lord Wellington would delay farther operations till it had capitulated; as he would then be enabled to bring forward a much greater body of troops into the field, and to leave the rear of his army open for the safe arrival of supplies.

The enemy retreated to a position in front of St. Jean de Luz, and drew up his lines upon a very strong range of heights covering that town, extending their left towards the mountain of Petite La Rhune, The whole front of this position was entrenched and defended by a series of remarkably strong redoubts, one behind the other. In rear of the village of Urogne, no less than five redoubts were constructed. In front of the centre of this part of his position, there is a small rivulet which empties itself into the Bay of St. Jean de Luz near Fort Socoa; this rivulet the enemy dammed up at its mouth, which caused a considerable inundation, greatly strengthening his front. A line was, as if by mutual consent, agreed upon for the positions of the outposts of the two armies, as soon as the action was over; the French keeping possession of the village of Urogne, and of a hill upon its right. A small chapel stands on this hill, and the French fortified it, and continued the line of entrenchments from thence to the sea. The most vulnerable points of the enemy's position, if any might be called so, on this part of his line, were strengthened by abbatis; and, as the country was well wooded and had numerous orchards, these defences were multiplied upon every part of his line. The cutting down of whole rows of orchard trees was a serious evil to the unfortunate inhabitants, who, however, had almost to a man fled the country; in ignorance of the protection which the Marquess of Wellington resolved to enforce, by the strictest severity of discipline in his army.

The first and fifth divisions, Lord Aylmer's brigade, and the Portuguese, encamped on the summit of the ridge, which had been previously occupied by the French. The Portuguese of Brigadier-General Wilson, upon the right, occupied a hutted camp, from which they had dislodged the enemy in the late engagement: their right communicated with the Spaniards under General Freyre on the Mountain of Mandalle, their left with the first division under Major-General Howard. Of this division, Colonel Maitland's brigade of Guards was on the right of the great road leading to Urogne, communicating with Major-General Hinuber's brigade of the King's German Legion upon its left. Upon the left of these was the second brigade of Guards, under Major-General Stopford, and the remainder of the ground, from thence to the sea, was occupied by the light German brigade, and by the fifth division, supported by a brigade of Portuguese encamped in front of Andaye. In these positions the Allies remained till after the surrender of Pamplona.

The view of the allied camp shows the range of hills occupied by the first and fifth divisions. It was taken from a conical hill, about mid-way between the mountain of Mandalle and the great road leading to Urogne, immediately upon the right of the hutted camp, occupied by Brigadier-General Wilson's Portuguese. In the distance may be seen the Bidassoa, near its mouth, with the extremity of Jaysquibel Mountain rising behind it. The town of Fontarabia is also discernible on the bank of the river. The Bay of Biscay bounds the horizon.

Chapter 3

Crossing the Nivelle

The unavoidable delay, occasioned by the necessity of waiting intelligence of the surrender of Pamplona, gave fresh opportunities to the officers of making excursions among the mountains, and of enjoying the magnificent and ever-varying scenery. The road along the banks of the Bidassoa now became the principal line of communication with, and that along which supplies of all kinds were conveyed to, the centre of the army. The valley through which this boundary river passes may justly be considered as affording some of the most romantic and beautiful scenery, perhaps, in all Europe, uniting, in a remarkable degree, the various characters of the sublime, the beautiful, and the picturesque. At every bend of the river, the road along its banks brings us suddenly on some new and striking feature. The pleasing combination of wood and rock, overhanging the beautifully winding stream, contrasted with the barren grandeur of the mountain summits, which tower above them, present an infinite number of the most delightful prospects. The oak, the chestnut, and the walnut, are the most conspicuous trees along the valley, and the slopes of the inferior hills; whilst, among the crevices of the rocks, the ever-green box tree grows with surprising luxuriance, and by its deep verdure relieves, while it contrasts in a very beautiful manner, the bright silver tints of the surrounding rocks, clothed with lichens. In sketching these picturesque scenes, and in making plans of the ground, several of the officers occupied themselves at such times as they were not engaged on military duty.

Following the direction of the valley, and about three miles above Irun, the road passes through a fine chestnut wood, covering the slope of the mountain, in which may every now and then be caught, through the openings, delightful views of the opposite steeps of Mandalle, and of the river winding through the vale below. The characteristic peculiarity of these scenes was frequently enlivened by the numerous little carts drawn by oxen, creaking through the valley, or by long, trains of muleteers, winding along the mountain paths, and singing their wild national airs, while conveying their loads of provisions to the camp. In the annexed view of the banks of the Bidassoa, some of the entrenchments, thrown up by the enemy to guard the banks of the river, appear on the sides of the opposite mountain. The advantage which the French must necessarily have had, when posted on the side of these steep heights, so difficult of access, adds not a little to the merit of the Spaniards, who so gallantly drove them from such a position.

Proceeding a little further, the valley becomes narrower; and the river is confined so closely between steep banks, as to have made it necessary to cut the road out of the solid rock. At the distance of about five miles above Irun, is a post-house, called Endarlacha, where there is a ford across the river. Almost directly opposite to this house, a mountain-torrent rushes down from the slopes of the Crown Mountain into the Bidassoa. This torrent marks the boundaries of Guipuscoa and Navarre, and its junction with the Bidassoa is about a hundred yards above the point where the line, drawn from the summit of La Rhune through Mont Commissari, meets the river, and defines the boundary between France and Spain. From hence to the mouth of the river below Fontarabia, the limits of the two nations are marked by the middle of its course. It might be supposed that, upon the very frontier, there could not be any very striking distinction between the inhabitants of the two sides: the case, however, is otherwise; a person no sooner crosses the limits, than he perceives a different race of people, a different style of buildings, different language and manners, bursting upon him all at once.

These opportunities of examining the character of the country were only obtained at intervals. The rainy season, which commenced soon after the left wing had established itself on the French territory, was against such excursions in the mountains; and shortly afterwards, the army began to experience the bad effects of its exposed situation. The days were frequently very hot, and generally succeeded by piercing cold frosty nights. Heavy rain usually followed, and continued, with little intermission, for several days and nights. The tents afforded but a bad protection, as the wind beat the rain through the canvass, and rendered the interior almost untenantable. On the right and centre of the army, the troops were even in a worse condition than those of the left wing, as they occupied positions nearer the centre of the Pyrenean chain, higher up the mountains and were, therefore, exposed to greater vicissitudes of temperature, and to the drizzling mists which almost constantly were hanging over their summits. The provisions, too, were far from being good. The cattle, driven up to the army through a great portion of Spain, arrived in a jaded and lean condition; the roads, along which they had been driven, might easily be traced by the numbers of their carcasses, lying half buried at their sides. It often happened that, within an hour after the oxen had been driven up to the camp, the meat was shared out, and cooked for the soldiers' messes.

Under such circumstances, it is not surprising that, at this period, whilst the most unremitting attention was required on the out-post duties, in the bleakest situations, and whilst, during the intervals the soldiers were labouring at the construction of redoubts and works of defence, many desertions should have taken place. They were, in fact, fewer than could have been expected. The mortality, however, was considerable, but not to be compared with that which, in 1512, carried off the greater part of the army of Francis I., (then Duke of Valois); nor to that which, in the Revolutionary War of 1794, compelled the left wing of the French army to retreat to St. Jean Pied de Port, being unable to withstand the inclement weather in the passes of the Pyrenees.

Owing to the heavy rains, the Bidassoa frequently ran so high as to render the fords totally impassable; and till the old bridge, sometimes called the Bridge of Beobie, or Behobie, which connects the great roads from Bayonne and Vittoria to Irun, was put into temporary repair, the communication was kept open by a pontoon bridge. Higher up, where the narrowness of the valley confined the river between its rocky banks, it became, in the rainy season, an impetuous torrent. The ford of Endarlacha, which we have before mentioned, was quite impracticable; and, to provide against emergencies, a floating bridge was established at that point.

It always happens that the inhabitants of the country which is the theatre of military operations unfortunately suffer, more or less, the calamities attendant on war; nor are they the less liable to be exposed to them on the part of their own countrymen carrying arms, than from their foreign allies. The various articles requisite for the support of an army, and the means resorted to, for enabling it to carry on its operations, are but too often of necessity to be sought for and procured upon the spot. In such cases, individual interest must be made to yield to the common cause. An instance of this sort occurred at the particular place here described. A little way above the confluence of the rivulet we have before mentioned, (which separates the provinces of Guipuscoa and Navarre,) there was a small iron foundry, apparently almost denying access to human beings, on account of the steepness of the rocky chasm in which it was situated. The appearance of its proprietor was almost as wild as his native abode, and his looks of despair are beyond description, when he beheld some artificers mercilessly plundering his machinery of its most valuable iron cramps and staples, for the construction of the temporary bridge at Endarlacha. He pleaded, but without effect; swore, but to no purpose; and at last wrung his hands, and called on a host of saints to the protection of his little property, on which the maintenance of his family depended. Individual hardships of this kind, severe as they are, and unjust as they may be considered, are unavoidable in a state of warfare; and when they are weighed in the scale of general expediency for the public good, and not wantonly inflicted, they may admit of, and are entitled to, an excuse. At this particular period, when the glorious struggle for national independence which Spain and Portugal, aided by their powerful ally, were on the eve of bringing to a successful termination, individual sacrifices were rendered of less moment, in the accomplishment of so important an object: the wonder is that they were not greater, when it is considered how long the Peninsula had been laid waste, and made desolate; and that millions of its unhappy inhabitants had been plundered and massacred by an inundation of hostile legions, whose course was almost every where marked by rapine and cruelty; and whose territory, in their turn, was now invaded. It may here, however, be observed, that the strict discipline kept up among the British troops, afforded few occasions to the inhabitants of Spain, or even of France, of complaint against them. The latter, however, had ample reason to expect, and they certainly did expect, a full measure of retaliation for all the evils which their countrymen had carried into the Peninsula. The Marquess of Wellington foresaw this, and provided against it by a general order to the following effect:

> The Commander of the Forces is particularly desirous that the inhabitants should be well treated. Officers and soldiers must recollect that their nations are at war with France solely because the ruler of the French nation will not allow them to be at peace, and is desirous of forcing them to submit to his yoke; and they must not forget that most of the evils suffered by the enemy, in his profligate invasion of Spain and Portugal, have been occasioned by the irregularities of his soldiers, and their cruelties, authorized and encouraged by their chiefs, towards the unfortunate and peaceful inhabitants of the country. To avenge this conduct upon the peaceable inhabitants of France would be unmanly, and unworthy of the nations to whom the Commander of the Forces now addresses himself.

There certainly was, however, a strong desire, more particularly on the part of the Spaniards and Portuguese, to inflict on the natives of France some of those evils which both nations had so severely felt at the hands of the French troops; and notwithstanding the humane order of the Marquess of Wellington, many outrages were committed, and sometimes under the immediate eye of the officers, without the latter using their authority to prevent them. But on this being made known to the Commander-in-Chief, he not only reiterated his former order, but reprimanded some, and sent others home to be dealt with as the Prince Regent might think fit, adding to his former order, that "the Commander of the Forces is determined not to command officers who will not obey his orders."

From this time, the most rigid discipline was observed, and the utmost respect paid to the persons and property of the enemy; so much so, that one of their own officers, in his Account of the peninsular war, is compelled to admit, that the combined armies treated the French with mildness, and paid for every article put under requisition, while his own countrymen made no ceremony in taking from the inhabitants whatever they wanted, without ever intending to pay for them; but then the English, he says, observed this good conduct, because they were afraid that, had they acted otherwise, they would have excited the indignation of his countrymen*.

The scenery at Endarlacha is remarkably picturesque, the sides of the mountains being here more than usually diversified with wood and rock. The post-house stands at the foot of the mountain on the right bank, close to the ford of the river, which is indicated in the annexed view by some figures crossing it. In this view, the mountain nearest on the right, stands in the province of Guipuscoa. The mountain forming the back ground in Navarre, whilst the rocky slope, on the left, shows the point which marks the frontiers of France and Spain. At the foot of the mountain opposite, the valley of the Bidassoa forms a sudden bend to the left, in the direction of Bera. It is here that the road to

---

* *Précis Historique de la Guerre d'Espagne et de Portugal, de 1808 à 1814.* Par Auguste Carel, Chef de Battaillon, &c.

Lezaca quits that which leads to Bera, by a long succession of zigzags to the summit of the opposite mountain; from which, there is a commanding prospect into the Valley of Cinco-villas, encircled by a range of lofty peaks, gradually increasing in height towards the centre of the chain.

The whole of the neighbouring country is rich in iron mines, and foundries for smelting the ore; and its inhabitants are chiefly employed in the manufacture of that metal. The district of the Cinco-villas is intersected by ridges of rocky mountains, separating the five towns, from which it takes its name, from each other. The chief town is Lezaca, where the Marquess of Wellington had his head-quarters, till the left wing of the army crossed the Bidassoa; he then removed to Bera. The whole district comprises a tract of country of about eighteen miles in length and nearly as many in width. It is traversed by the Bidassoa, and communicates with the fertile valley of Bastan along the direction of the river, which, emerging from this valley, takes a large sweep round the base of the mountain of Atalza by St. Estevan in the Valley of Lerins, and then assuming a northern course, enters this district.

The Valley of Bastan, at the head of which the Bidassoa takes its rise, is the most populous tract of country which borders on that river: its inhabitants have been estimated at seven thousand. Maya, situated near the head of the valley, is called a royal town the remaining two are named Elissondo and Irrueta. Besides several villages, there are numerous villas scattered over the whole of this romantic and beautiful valley. It was here that the Biscayan merchants were wont to retire from active business, to enjoy the delights of rural life; and hence a degree of opulence was still visible in the appearance of the peasantry around, not usually seen in such secluded and mountainous regions. It abounds in rich pasturage and productive orchards, but the vine is rarely seen. Prior to the war, it was well stocked with sheep and horned cattle. The mountains which bound this valley, consist of a lofty range, enveloping it on all sides, except on that which borders, the course of the Bidassoa. By these mountains it is separated, on the north; from the Pays de Labourt; on the west; from the Cinco-villas; on the south, from the Valley of Lanz; and on the east, from the Valley of Los Aldudes and Baygorry, by the steep ridge of the Mountain of Haussa. The highest point of this ridge is elevated upwards of four thousand feet above the level of the sea. Many of those who took delight in mountain scenery, and few there are who are not impressed with that feeling, sometimes were tempted to prolong their rambles beyond what strict prudence would have warranted. The Pyrenean chain can scarcely be said to have been examined by the botanist or geologist. A few notices are given by Townsend, but Raymond and La Perouse are the only two who have ascended the highest summits with a view to scientific information. The two highest points in the chain are Mont Perdu and Canigou; the former being nearly eleven thousand feet above the surface of the sea, and the other not much lower. From these peaked summits, towards each extremity of the chain, the height of the mountains declines to the Bay of Biscay and the Mediterranean; the declination to the latter being much more precipitous than that towards the Bay of Biscay, owing to their proximity to the Mediterranean; whereas the slope towards the Bay of Biscay is marked by the gradual decrease of elevation in the successive mountains of Somme de Soube, elevated about ten thousand feet; Pic du Midi, about nine thousand; Pic d'Anie, or Ahunga, about seven thousand seven hundred; Mont de Hory, about six thousand two hundred; Mont d'Orsansurietta, about four thousand eight hundred Mont de Haussa, about four thousand; Mont la Rhune, about two thousand eight hundred; and Jaysquibel, about one thousand seven hundred feet above the level of the sea. A continuous ridge of mountain may be traced, connecting the western extremity of the Pyrenees with the Sierras of the north of Spain and the great chain of the Asturias.

The great body of the Pyrenean chain is unquestionably of primitive formation; but masses of secondary limestone so completely superincumb the granite, porphyry, and other primitive rock, and particularly on the side next to France, that La Peyrouse, on seeing the numerous impressions of marine animals, and other organic remains, supposes the very highest points to have yielded to the fury of the ocean, which has left only the secondary formations visible. Among the calcareous masses are beautiful specimens of a rose-coloured marble with white spots. These masses rise on the sides of Mont Perdu in walls, almost perpendicular, to the height of five or six hundred feet; so as to make the ascent nearly impracticable. The summit of this peak is covered with perpetual snow; but the extremities of the chain are free from snow, except sometimes in the depth of winter. The fertile side of the chain is that which faces France, owing, as Townsend supposes, to the superincumbent limestone, whilst the opposite or Spanish side, mostly of primitive rock, exhibits a more barren appearance.

One of the most pleasing scenes of the Valley of the Bidassoa is at the point where the road to Lezaca from Irun quits the margin of the river, and gives a view of its course where it bends in the direction of Bera. No trace of human habitation is visible at this point; the river ripples beautifully over a bed of rocks, and its banks are luxuriantly skirted with wood. Crossing the river at the ford of Endarlacha, and pursuing the road to Bera, we obtain another striking view of this romantic vale. The peculiarity of the prospect was heightened by a long train of Spaniards carrying officers and soldiers to the rear, who had been wounded in the late engagements, and who were always removed to proper hospitals as soon as it could be done with safety. The care of the sick and wounded necessarily employed a number of men; and they could no where receive such able attention as in the general hospitals established within the Spanish frontiers. The rugged mountain road was not passable for the spring-wagons, on which the wounded are usually conveyed to the rear; and they were therefore carried in blankets, fastened at the sides to a couple, of poles, and thus borne on the shoulders of the peasantry. This mode of conveyance on bad roads is far preferable to that of the spring-wagons, but as it required four men to carry one sick person, the transport of a small number of them gave the train a formidable appearance, when seen extended for so great a length along, the windings of the mountain track.

Whilst the left wing remained encamped on the heights in front of Urogne, an event occurred, which, though trifling in importance, excited considerable interest in the troops who were witnesses of it. A French gun-brig was discovered by one of our cruisers coasting the bay between the mouth of the Adour and St. Jean de Luz. It was a beautiful morning. The plains of France were visible to a great extent, and the Bay of Biscay was gently ruffled by a light breeze. The English squadron could be discerned in the offing, but a schooner had contrived to beat up within gunshot of the enemy, and a brisk cannonade was kept up for a considerable time from both vessels. All eyes were turned eagerly to witness the result of this little combat, which took place within view of both the hostile armies. The result was cheering to the allied troops, for, after the firing had been kept up for some time, the French took to their boats and set fire to the vessel, to prevent its falling into the hands of the English. As the flames continued to spread, the guns, which had been left loaded, got heated, and fired off from time to time; at length she blew up, scattering masts and spars to a great distance around. The smoke caused by the explosion assumed the singular appearance of a large tree with roots, stem, and umbrageous branches. It was so dense that the light breezes were a long time in dispersing it. The disparity of force between the two vessels, and the disgraceful result of this little exploit, must have proved highly mortifying to the French army. The name of the French vessel, we afterwards learnt, was the *Fulibistier.*

Towards the close of October, and during the first week in November, the French were seen making great exertions to complete their defensive works. Opposite to the allied left wing the nature of these defences appeared of the most formidable kind; and, to judge by appearances, it would cost little less than the storming of a regular fortification, were an attack made upon this part of the enemy's line. Marshal Soult was, doubtless, aware of the distressed state of the garrison of Pamplona, and, therefore, might look forward to its immediate surrender, and the consequent advance of the Allies. He had failed in every attempt for its relief, and during the whole period of the blockade was never able to hold communication with it. At length, after a blockade of four months, the garrison of Pamplona, having exhausted the whole of its provisions, surrendered on the 31st of October, and liberated the covering army for the prosecution of its intended career in France.

Preparations were immediately made for attacking the enemy. On the 7th of November several brigades of artillery crossed the Bidassoa, and took post in rear of the left wing. In the evening orders arrived for the troops to be formed in marching order at three o'clock the following morning; two days' provisions were served out, and all looked with interest for the approaching contest of the morrow.

Heavy rains, however, had fallen during the night, and rendered the ground so thoroughly soaked, as to be in many places, quite impassable for artillery. A counter order was, therefore, given, that "The intended movements were not to take place." But the weather proving more favourable on the 8th and 9th, a fresh order arrived on the evening of the latter day, to be in readiness at three the following morning.

We have already noticed the positions occupied by the right wing of the French in front of the allied left. The entrenchments on that part of the enemy's line were considered too strong for an attack in front*. Lord Wellington, therefore, resolved on attacking the centre and left. But there also the French had guarded their position by a very strong line of redoubts and entrenchments; their centre, by works constructed on the range of heights between the great mountain of La Rhune and the banks of the Nivelle; their left, by works constructed on the heights of Ainhouë, on the right bank of that river, and farther strengthened also by entrenchments on its left bank, to connect them with the chain of works covering the centre. The whole of this entrenched position is laid down upon the plan.

Immediately after the passage of the Bidassoa, the command of the left wing was entrusted to Lieutenant-General Sir John Hope. The gallant Sir Thomas Graham had returned to England to take charge of an expedition destined to assist in the liberation of Holland. The troops looked up with confidence and with veneration to their new commander, whose high reputation for military skill, and whose example of personal intrepidity, were well known in the army to have been displayed on all occa-

* Lord Wellington's Despatches, dated St. Pé, November 13, 1813. "The enemy, not satisfied with the natural strength of this position, had the whole of it fortified; and their right, in particular, had been made so strong, that I did not deem it expedient to attack it in front."

sions. Lord Wellington's arrangements for the intended attack were, of course, unknown, except to the general and staff officers, and the assault of the enemy's strong lines of redoubts, which, on the morning of the 10th, all expected to be engaged in, seemed an operation of great hazard, and one that was likely to cause prodigious havoc in the assailing columns.

The troops, having formed upon their parades soon after three o'clock, began descending from the heights where they had been so long encamped, and silently advanced to the verge of the line of out-picquets, where they arrived, each brigade at their appointed station, about an hour before dawn. It was a most beautiful moonlight morning, and so clear that it was difficult to say at which moment night ended and day began. The troops were ordered to lay down on the ground, and great caution was observed to avoid making any noise, which might intimate the approaching attack to the enemy. Nothing can be more interesting than the period when an army awaits in silent expectation the signal for battle. As dawn gradually broke over the landscape, objects became more discernible, and columns might be seen at various distances, screened from the enemy's view by little eminences or woods.

During this pause the plan for the ensuing operation was whispered about. It appeared that the Field Marshal's intention was to occupy the attention of the enemy with the display of his left wing, and by feint attacks made against the right wing of the French, to withdraw their attention as much as possible from their centre and left wing; whilst, with his right wing and centre, he should force through the chain of redoubts and entrenchments opposed to him; and thus, by establishing himself in rear of the French right wing, oblige it to abandon the strong position covering St. Jean de Luz and the lower part of the Nivelle. It was even hoped, should the event prove successful, and sufficient time be gained for so extended a movement, that the columns of the right and centre might be pushed so far forward as to intercept the retreat of a great portion of the French right wing, which, by protracting its defence of that part of the fortified position, would hazard its line of communication with Bayonne.

On the 6th of November the second division, under Lieutenant-General the Honourable Sir William Stewart, which formed the right of the Allies in the Pass of Roncesvalles, was moved to Maya in the Valley of Bastan, where Lieutenant-General Sir Rowland Hill concentrated the remainder of the right wing, consisting of the sixth division, under Lieutenant-General Sir Henry Clinton; Lieutenant-General Sir John Hamilton's Portuguese division; General Morillo's Spanish division; and the thirteenth and fourteenth Light Dragoons, under Colonel Grant, and a proportionate force of artillery.

The right of the centre, formed of the third, fourth, and seventh divisions, respectively under the orders of Major-General the Honourable Charles Colville, Lieutenant-General the Honourable Sir Lowry Cole, and Mariscal de Campo (Major-General,) Le Cor, was assembled under the orders of Marshal Sir William Beresford, and concentrated for the attack in the valleys between the great mountain of La Rhune and the Pass of Etchalar.

The light division commanded by Major-General Charles Baron Alten, formed the left centre supported by Brigadier-General Longa's , corps of Spaniards, and assembled for the attack in front of the Pass of Bera on the left of Mont La Rhune. The intermediate space, between the right and left centre, was occupied by the Spanish army of reserve, under Mariscal de Campo Don Pedro Giron.

The intermediate space, between the left of the centre and the left wing of the army, was occupied by the Spaniards under Lieutenant-General Don Manuel Freyre.

The left wing, under Lieutenant-General Sir John Hope, consisting of the first division, under Major-General Howard, and the fifth division under Major-General Hay, with Lord Aylmer's brigade, occupied the whole space from thence to the sea. The positions, occupied by the several columns preparatory to the attack, and the lines of march of each division during the action, are indicated on the plan.

Lieutenant-General Sir Stapleton Cotton, commanding in chief the cavalry of the army, supported the centre with Major-General Victor Alten's brigade of light cavalry. And Major-General Vandeleur's brigade, consisting of the twelfth and sixteenth Light Dragoons, supported the right of the first division, and a part of the heavy brigade of cavalry of the King's German Legion, its left.

A little to the left of the great road leading to Urogne, and a very short way in advance of that village, there is a rising ground connected with the range of hills where the allied left wing had been encamped by a ridge of hill extending in a direction nearly parallel with the great road. Upon this hill stood the ruins of a small chapel, around which the French had constructed a redoubt, and connected it with the defences of Urogne by entrenchments and a strong abbatis. This work formed a sort of advanced post to the French right wing, and the picquets posted opposite to it were always of great strength, and had a support of four hundred men commanded by a field officer, stationed close in the rear. A battery was thrown up on the ridge of hill we have just described, within a very short distance of the French redoubt and here Sir John Hope with his staff came to superintend the attack on the enemy's outposts on the morning of the 10th of November.

A short while before sunrise some artillery was brought up into the entrenchment, and almost instantaneously after, the whole line was aroused into action by the flash of the first cannon fired against the chapel redoubt. The enemy immediately answered it by a brisk fire from the redoubt, and a warm cannonade was kept up for some time on both sides. At the same signal the whole line of picquets commenced a smart attack upon the French outposts, and as our situation was well adapted for seeing the engagement to a great extent, the scene became extremely animated and interesting. The artillery having nearly silenced that of the enemy in the redoubt, Colonel Halket's brigade of Light German Infantry moved round the hill to the left, menacing the rear of the French, whilst Lieutenant-Colonel West, of the first Foot Guards, who was field officer in command of the picquets, made a brisk attack in front. The French still kept up a hot fire of musketry from the entrenchments, and from the abbatis; but the troops, rushing forward at the same moment, were soon in possession of the enemy's post, and drove him down the hill to the verge of the strong fortified position.

The ground between this hill and the sea was occupied by the second brigade of Guards, under Major-General Stopford, and the fifth division. The light troops of the different brigades drove in the enemy's picquets in their front. The village, or little town, of Urogne was attacked and carried by the eighty-fifth regiment of Major-General Lord Aylmer's Brigade; and on this point being carried, the fifth division pushed forward to the inundations, which covered the entrenchments in front of Ciboure, and those protecting the heights in advance of Fort Socoa. Sir John Hope directed a brisk cannonade to be kept up against the enemy's line, and by the spirit with which it was answered, it was evident that the French apprehended the onset would be followed up by an assault of their position. Whilst the attack against Urogne and the entrenchments on the left was going on, Major-General Howard directed the movements of the first brigade of Guards, under Colonel Maitland, and the brigade of line battalions of the King's German Legion, under Major-General Hinuber, against the formidable entrenchments which covered the heights immediately behind Urogne, and extended along the hills in the direction of Ascain. The German Legion Brigade was on the left near Urogne, the Guards on the right, and upon the right of these was the Portuguese brigade of Brigadier-General Wilson, contiguous to the road leading from Bera through the Pass of that name to St. Jean de Luz. A line, drawn from St. Jean de Luz to Bera, would intersect the point to which the extreme right of the left wing extended. Opposite to this point, the French had constructed a remarkably strong redoubt, to cover the approach to their position by the Bera road. A brigade of artillery took post on a hill directly opposite to it, and a hot fire of shot and shells was kept up for the greater part of the day against the redoubt; but the enemy tenaciously defended this point, although we could discern that they were suffering greatly from the fire of our artillery.

Throughout the greater part of the day a continued skirmish was kept up by the light companies of the German brigade, and by those of the first brigade of Guards, compelling the French to retreat within their breast-works and other entrenchments.

Meantime, the grand and principal manoeuvres of the day had been going on successfully upon the right and centre; and as the day advanced, we could distinguish afar off the allied columns ascending and attacking the entrenchments, which covered the French centre and left. The operations of the right wing commenced, by Sir Rowland Hill directing an attack upon the enemy's entrenchments on the left bank of the Nivelle, which covered the left wing of the French army in its position on the heights of Ainhouë; the Spaniards, under Morillo, moving at the same time, by the right bank of the river, against the village of that name.

The centre, under Marshal Beresford, advanced against the French centre in the camp of Sarre, and commenced, by the fourth division, under Sir Lowry Cole, attacking at day-break the redoubt in front of the right of that village, whilst the seventh division, under Mariscal de Campo Le Cor attacked that in front of the left. These points being carried, the fourth division attacked the village in front, whilst Major-General Colville moved round its left with the third division, and General Giron round its right with the Spanish reserve. This primary movement having proved successful, Sir Lowry Cole, with the fourth division, and General Giron with the Spaniards upon his left, attacked the centre of the strong fortified position behind Sarré, about Midway between Ascain and the banks of the Nivelle. The seventh division, under General Le Cor, and the third, under General Colville, at the same time attacked the left of the French centre, in the redoubts resting upon the Nivelle, whilst the light division, under Baron Alten, supported on its left by Brigadier-General Longa's Spaniards, co-operated by an attack upon the right centre of the enemy in the redoubts opposite the mountain of La Petite la Rhune: the entrenchments upon it having been previously assaulted and carried by the light division.

Lieutenant-General Don Manuel Freyre moved along the intermediate space between the left centre of the Allies, and their left wing, in the direction of Ascain.

The annexed view of Mont La Rhune is from the verge of the Mountain of Mandalle, on the side nearest to the Pass of Bera: the troops at this outpost were a part of General Freyre's corps; and in the valleys between it and Great La Rhune, some of the camps of the light division may be seen. The pointed summit of the opposite mountain is that of Great La Rhune; the rugged ridge to the left shows the portion of La Petite La Rhune which had been entrenched by the enemy; and the ravine or valley between these marks, the boundary between the French and the Allies, till the attack of the 10th of November; and it was in this ravine, separating the summits of Great and Little La Rhune, that Major-General Alten assembled his division preparatory to the attack.

The enemy, by a tenacious defence of one of his redoubts in the centre against a most daring attack on its front by the fifty-second regiment, under Colonel Colborne, gave time for the troops under Marshal Beresford to get so far into its rear, that retreat became impracticable; and the result was, the capture of a whole French battalion of the eighty-eighth regiment, nearly six hundred strong. The indignation of the French, on finding themselves prisoners, burst forth in the most violent and indecent exclamations; one of the sergeants in particular, decorated with the cross of the Legion d'Honneur, raved at being captured in a ——— redoute, after having been present in the splendid victories of Austerlitz and Wagram.

Every where the movements were attended with success, and, considering the formidable nature of the entrenchments, with comparatively very small loss. Marshal Soult, apparently, did not discover the object of the Marquess of Wellington's manoeuvres till late in the day, as it was not till one o'clock in the afternoon that he detached a division of his army from his right wing to support his centre; but this reinforcement arrived too late, and the Allies pursued their success, by crossing the Nivelle, and separating the French centre from their left wing.

The second and sixth divisions, under Sir William Stewart and Sir Henry Clinton, with the Portuguese division, under Sir John Hamilton, having crossed the Nivelle, attacked the French left wing, in the strong fortified position behind Ainhouë. Their attacks were chiefly directed against the entrenchments and redoubts resting upon the Nivelle, so as to neutralize the extreme left of the enemy in front of Souraide, and on the mountain of Mondarin. These attacks were conducted with great gallantry, the Allies successively dislodging the French from the three redoubts contiguous to the Nivelle. Sir Rowland Hill then directed a portion of these troops to push forward in the direction of Souraide and Espelette, and by their means compelled the extreme left of the enemy to take refuge in the mountains in the direction of St. Jean Pied de Port.

The centre of the Allies crossed the Nivelle opposite St. Pé; and thus the Marquess of Wellington accomplished his object, in establishing a considerable portion of the allied army in rear of the French right wing. From the great extent of the movements, and the extreme ruggedness of some parts of the ground, over which the Allies advanced in the different lines of march, together with the length of time requisite for the various attacks on the enemy's entrenchments, it was found impossible to follow up the successful issue of the battle by penetrating farther in his rear; and night put an end to the pursuit of the broken columns of the enemy's centre and left. The columns of the Allies, therefore, bivouacked, during the night, on the ground they had so gallantly won.

The successful result of the battle was owing, in no inconsiderable degree, to the able direction of the artillery under Colonel Dickson. Guns were brought to bear on the French fortifications from situations which they considered totally inaccessible to that arm. Mountain guns on swivel carriages, harnessed on the backs of mules, purposely trained for that service, ascended the rugged ridges of the mountains, and showered destruction on the entrenchments below. The foot and horse artillery displayed a facility of movement which must have astonished the French; the artillery-men dragging the guns with ropes up steep precipices, or lowering them down to positions, from whence they could, with more certain aim, pour forth their fatal vollies against the enemy.

A naval demonstration was made throughout the day, opposite to Fort Socoa, at the entrance of the harbour of St. Jean de Luz, by the Vesuvius, Challenger, Sparrow, and Racer, of the squadron under Sir George Collier; but the swell on this dangerous coast would not admit of a close approach. The French, however, fired several shot from the batteries contiguous to the sea, some of which struck the Sparrow.

It is not meant here to enter into any detail of the gallantry and judicious conduct with which the several attacks, in this brilliant affair, were conducted by the general officers of the different divisions and brigades; or of the intrepidity with which their example was followed, and their orders executed, by the respective officers and the brave soldiers whom they commanded; but it may be permitted to mention some of the names of the most distinguished of the killed and wounded. Major-General Byng, leading his brigade of the second division, was wounded; and also Major-General Kempt, commanding a brigade of the light division. Colonel Barnard, of the ninety-fifth regiment, whose talents as a leader of light troops are well known, was severely wounded. The gallant Colonel Lloyd, of the ninety-fourth, "an officer who had frequently distinguished himself, and was of great promise",* was unfortunately killed. Lieutenant-Colonel

* Lord Wellington's Despatches.

Rooke, of the third Guards, Assistant Adjutant-General; Lieutenant-Colonel Thornton, of the fortieth; Lieutenant-Colonel M'Donald, of the first battalion, fifty-seventh; and Lieutenant-Colonel Gough, of the eighty-seventh, were all severely wounded; as was also Lieutenant-Colonel M'Neal, serving with the tenth Portuguese regiment of the line, in Sir John Hamilton's division.

The total loss of the British and Portuguese, in killed, wounded, and missing, did not amount to more than two thousand six hundred officers and men, which, in the exaggerated statement of Monsieur Carel, is set down at four thousand.

The perfection, to which the experience of the long war in the Peninsula had brought the duties of the Adjutant-General's department, under the Honourable Sir Edward Pakenham; and that of the Quarter-Master-General, under Sir George Murray; the former in the extreme accuracy of its orders and regulations, and the latter in its precision in calculating and arranging the various movements, and in reconnoitring the country and taking up the several positions, formed, without doubt, the ground-work on which the success of the campaign, in a most material degree, depended. Joined to these, when we consider the high state of discipline of the troops, the ability and experience of their gallant leaders, all united under the command of the invincible Wellington, we may be pardoned for asserting, that the army in every operation against the enemy moved forward with a well-grounded confidence of success; indeed, to such a pitch had their confidence arrived, that the order for a fresh engagement was considered as little less than an order to gain a fresh victory.

The result of the day's operations was the retreat of the French right wing, during the night, from its position in front of St. Jean de Luz and the Lower Nivelle; leaving about fifty pieces of cannon in the works, which had cost them so much labour in erecting, and the taking of about fifteen hundred prisoners. The enemy destroyed a portion of the bridge which unites the town of Ciboure, or Siboure, on the left bank of the Nivelle, with St. Jean de Luz, upon the right bank; besides all the bridges of communication which had been established between that town and the vicinity of St. Pé; so that Sir John Hope was unable to press upon the retiring columns on the road towards Bayonne.

Early on the morning of the 11th, the left wing got under arms; but it was near eight o'clock before the first division advanced towards the banks of the Nivelle, the repairs of the bridge at St. Jean de Luz, and the construction of a flying bridge to assist in conveying the troops over, occupied the artificers a considerable time, so that it was mid-day before they were rendered passable for artillery, and the march was consequently delayed till this was effected. About half-past twelve the columns of the fifth division, and the second brigade of Guards, passed the Neville at St. Jean de Luz, part by fords close above the town, and part, with the artillery, over the bridge. The first division passed at a ford about a mile higher up the river, together with the Portuguese brigade of Brigadier-General Wilson. It rained torrents the whole forenoon, but the spectacle of the allied columns descending from the fortified position in files to the banks of the river, and then forming columns in the most perfect order; with the grand style in which the troops forded the river and ascended the opposite bank, was remarkably striking. The ford was broad enough to cross by platoons, and though the water was deep, and the right bank exceedingly muddy, all passed in high spirits. Many of the soldiers' wives were seen wading through the river and dragging themselves through the muddy banks and swampy ground of the opposite shore by the sides of the companies to which their husbands belonged. The more sanguine looked forward to penetrating at once into the interior of France. At night the left wing bivouacked on a ridge of hills extending from Guethary in the direction of Espelette, the enemy having retreated to the neighbourhood of Bidart. On the following day tents and camp equipage arrived, but the rain of the 11th was, only the commencement of bad weather, which continued without intermission till the 18th of November, rendering the cross roads so muddy and bad, besides swelling all the rivulets into broad and deep streams, that any attempts to advance farther at that period must have faded. The Marquess of Wellington, in consequence, moved the army on the 18th of November into cantonments; the first division occupying St. Jean de Luz and Ciboure, with the village of Guethary in advance.

In the view of St. Jean de Luz, and the banks of the Nivelle from Ciboure, may be discovered the whole course of the lower Nivelle; and, as the view is towards the interior, part of the Pyrenean chain bounds the horizon. The houses on the right in this view area part of Ciboure; the greater portion of the town is, however, screened from view by the rising ground in front. On the left, part of the town of St. Jean de Luz is seen. In the centre of the view is an island, formed by the spreading of the Nivelle just above the towns. The island is connected by bridges with Ciboure and St. Jean de Luz, and it was over these bridges that the right wing of the enemy retreated in the night between the 10th and 11th of November, the French rear guard partly destroying them before quitting St. Jean de Luz. Higher up the river is a trestle bridge, which was constructed by our artificers on the site of one which the French had constructed, and afterwards destroyed in their retreat; it was at this point that the greater part of the first division and the Portuguese, attached to it, forded the river on the 11th; and the low swampy ground, extending from the water's edge to the right bank of the river, may be seen to the left of the island.

Formerly Ciboure was connected with St. Jean de Luz by one continued bridge, without touching the island; some of the piers of this bridge are still visible at low water. In the year 1636, this bridge was the scene of an obstinate combat between the French rear-guard and the Spaniards. In the history of the life of the Duke of Espernon, Governor of Guienne, we find that his son, the Duke de la Valette, rode from Bayonne to St. Jean de Luz, on hearing of the invasion of the Pays de Labourt by the Spaniards, whose rapid advance, however, only gave him time to entrust the defence of the bridge of St. Jean de Luz to La Roche, Captain of the Duke d'Espernon's guards, with a view to cover the retreat of the few troops which could be assembled. The account of the affair is thus given in Cotton's translation.

> The Duke de la Valette engaged his person so far to make good this retreat, and to preserve the little honour he had to manage in this encounter, that he very often ran a very great hazard of his life, and certainly exposed himself more than he was any way obliged to do, when being in the end retired, (himself always the last man), he commanded La Roche, Captain of the Duke, his father's guards, and also of his own, to make good the bridge (which separates the Bourg of Siboure from that of St. Jean de Luz) against the enemy that followed very close in his rear. This order was not to be executed without infinite danger, but the Duke de la Valette well enough knew, that he, to whom it was given, would not belie his former actions; neither did La Roche deceive his expectation, who, with forty musketeers only, which he had under his com-

mand, stopped the torrent of a victorious army; and after having killed two hundred of their men upon the place, amongst whom were eight or ten of their best officers, and having by that means given our foot time to put themselves into a place of safety; after he had sufficiently manifested his own conduct, with the valour and dexterity of his soldiers, he drew up the draw-bridge that lay over the middle of the river, and with very little loss retired to the Duke de la Valette's troop, who staid to make good his retreat.

Chapter 4

St. Jean de Luz

As soon as the army had gone into cantonments, the Marquess of Wellington established his head-quarters at St. Jean de Luz. The first and second brigades of Guards were cantoned in that town and in the suburb of Ciboure. For the greater convenience and despatch, a printing-press was established in the large building on the island, which connects the two parts of the bridge across the Nivelle, from which printed orders were distributed to every part of the allied army.

The enemy having withdrawn the great body of his forces within an entrenched camp, in front of Bayonne, the Marquess adopted the precautionary measure of forming a line of out-posts, for the protection of the allied cantonments. The right and centre of the army guarded the left bank of the Nive, by occupying Cambo, Larressore, Ustaritz, and Arrauntz, turning to the left *en potence* in front of Arcangues, opposite a chateau of the Senator Garrat. The left wing held a line of out-posts in continuation to the sea-coast, between Bidart and Biarits, crossing the great Bayonne road at the house of Barouillet, the residence of the Mayor of Biarits. Two small lakes defended the front of this portion of the line; the Etang de Chuhigue, the front of the Plateau of Barouillet and the Etang de Rousta, the

Plateau of Bassussary. The great Bayonne road leads across a valley between these lakes, and here was the most advanced line of sentinels guarding the left wing.

St. Jean de Luz, though built on a very flat piece of ground, nearly level with the surface of the Nivelle at high water, is so situated as to afford a very picturesque view. The Nivelle, dividing the town from Ciboure, enters a beautiful semicircular bay, which takes its name from St. Jean de Luz. This semicircle is terminated on the north-east by a rocky point of land, on which a battery was erected, named from an adjoining chapel, Fort Ste. Barbe. A short pier extends in a direction crossing the entrance to the bay from this point. The opposite side of the bay is terminated in the south-west by the harbour and Fort of Soma, where there is also a short pier extending in a direction which crosses the entrance to the bay, and corresponding with the pier of Ste. Barbe. The width of the bay, from Fort Ste. Barbe to Fort Socoa, is very nearly one English mile. These piers, however, extend but a short distance, and afford little or no security to vessels at anchor in the bay. They were originally intended to have been carried nearly across it, and to have had light-houses erected on their extreme points, between which a sufficiently wide entrance to the harbour would still have been left. This grand project, besides affording secure anchorage to vessels trading on this stormy coast, would have added to the security of St. Jean de Luz against the violent force the sea, which, in very heavy gales, threatens the total destruction of the town. Fear the better protection of the town, however, a strong wall has been built, skirting that side of it which adjoins the bay, and extends nearly its whole length. The top of this wall is wide enough to afford an excellent promenade for the inhabitants, and it slopes from thence into the sea, so as to break the force of the waves by its inclination. This barrier wall was in part broken down by a tremendous storm in the year 1777, which caused the destruction of many houses, and threatened the submersion of the whole town.

The esplanade, on the summit of this wall, was a favourite walk of the Marquess of Wellington, who might there be seen in a plain grey coat, devoid of all military parade and attendance, enjoying a momentary relaxation from the bustle and cares of the camp. On the retreat of the French army, the inhabitants of St. Jean de Luz had generally remained shut up in their houses, waiting in trembling anxiety for the moment when, as they had been told, or had persuaded themselves, they would be plundered of their property and maltreated in every possible way by the conquerors; but when they were informed that the most rigid orders were given for the protection of person and property, they gradually, but cautiously, began to show themselves abroad. They soon, however, gained confidence, opened their shops, and followed their usual occupations. It was amusing to observe with what amazement they regarded the affability of manner, and the unassuming style of dress, of the British Commander-in-Chief; so different to what they had been accustomed in the French generals, strutting about in splendid uniforms, attended every where by the staff officers and their aides-de-camp.

The houses of St. Jean de Luz consist for the most part of long low buildings, whose gable ends, with large projecting roofs, front the principal street, called La Grande Rue. Wooden balconies are carried across the fronts of most of the buildings, which render the ground floors very dark and gloomy, and fit only for lumber rooms. The Grande Rue extends from the entrance of the town on the Bayonne side as far as the Hotel de Ville, which fronts the market-place opposite to the quay. In, this part of the town there are some large houses, built partly in the French and partly in the Spanish style. In the annexed view of the quay may be remarked a large building, having arcades in front of the middle stories; it was occupied by the heads of the Commissariat department. The house beyond was inhabited by the Adjutant-General Sir Edward Pakenham, whose memory will long be revered by the-army, and by his countrymen. In the back ground, part of Ciboure is seen fronting the little harbour.

The trade and commercial activity of St. Jean de Luz have long fallen to decay. The inhabitants of the surrounding country (the Pays de Labourt) were, in former times, famous for their daring enterprises in long sea voyages; and it is well known that they were among the earliest to venture upon the hazardous employment of the northern whale fishery. The preference which they still give to commercial, rather than agricultural, pursuits, is visible in the small portion of the population scattered over the interior of the country; a very considerable part of its surface, capable of cultivation, still remaining in a state of nature. The treaty of 1763 between France and England, by which the former lost a great part of her Transatlantic possessions, gave a death-blow to the naval prosperity of St. Jean de Luz, which is now rarely frequented by vessels of larger tonnage than the coasting *chasse-marées* of the adjoining provinces. There is still, however, a *chantier de construction* on the island between the bridges, where sloops and small brigantines are occasionally built.

In describing the Bidassoa, an allusion was made to the celebrated treaty of the Pyrenees, negotiated in the Isle of Pheasants. The conferences were conducted by Cardinal Mazarine on the part of France, and Don Luis Mendez de Haro on that of Spain, from the 13th of August to the 7th of November, 1659, when Maria Teresa, daughter of Philip IV., was contracted to Louis XIV. The marriage was solemnized in the Hôtel de Ville of St. Jean de Luz, on the 9th of June, 1660. In the annexed view, which is taken from the island in the Nivelle, may be seen the Hôtel de Ville, just beyond the bridge; it is distinguished by its turreted angles and arcaded windows.

The town, or suburb, of Ciboure is not much inferior in size to St. Jean de Luz; it consists, however, of only two principal streets; the one in the direction towards the Spanish frontier; the other, which is very narrow, extending along the left bank of the Nivelle, where it enters the Bay of St. Jean de Luz, by a narrow channel, confined between stone piers.

From the 18th of November to the 9th of December, no general movement of the army took place. Partial reencounters, however, occurred occasionally. A reconnaissance was made by the French of the positions occupied by the left wing on the 18th of November; General Wilson's Portuguese brigade held the enemy in check, and during the skirmish that general was wounded. On the 19th of November, the enemy made an unsuccessful attempt to drive in the advance of the allied centre, which, on the former day, crossed the bridge of Urdains in front of Bassussarry, and guarded the road which, leading from Bayonne, branches off at that point towards Ste. Pé and Ustaritz. On the 23d of November, the advance of the light division imprudently pushed forwards to the entrenched camp before Bayonne, and was driven back to its proper line, with the loss of about ninety men and officers, in killed, wounded, and prisoners. The right wing of the army had remained stationary since its passage of the Nivelle; the only encounter on that part of the line was at Cambo on the Nive, where the enemy occupied a *tête de pont*, but, having been attacked on the 16th of November, withdrew behind that river, and destroyed the bridge.

The occupation of these positions gave the Allies possession of a great portion of the Pays de Labourt, which forms a part of that country, which was known to the Romans under the name of Cantabria; and whose inhabitants, taking refuge in the fastnesses of the Pyrenean mountains, for a long series of years maintained their independence against the attacks of the Roman legions. Various authors have described the countries inhabited by the ancient Cantabrians, but their accounts of this peculiar race of people, and the extent of their territory, are often at variance; some excluding whole provinces, whilst others give them an extension of limits beyond what appears, by all the records that remain, to have belonged to them. They seem anciently to have occupied the whole tract of country now comprised in the Provinces of Biscay, Alava, and Guipuzcoa; besides a great part of the kingdom of Navarre; the Pays de Labourt and the Bearnois, forming a considerable portion of Aquitania.[1] As a part of the inhabitants of Aquitania[2], they were found to be among the most formidable opponents whom the Roman generals had to encounter, but they were totally defeated by P. Crassus[3]; and, afterwards, when Caesar visited Aquitania[4], he received hostages for their submission. Under Augustus, the Cantabrians made a fresh effort to shake off the Roman yoke. For a long time they held out against the Imperial arms, till Agrippa was sent with a powerful army to subjugate the country. At length, they were so hemmed in by the Romans, that, for want of provisions, they were compelled to try the fate of a general

1. Concerning the Aquitanians in Gaul, it is certain that they were of Iberian or Cantabrian blood. – Adelung's *Mithridates*, vol. ii.

2. J. Cæsar., de Bello Gallico, lib. i. – *Aquitania à Garumna flumine ad Pyræneos montes et eam partem Oceani quæ ad Hispaniam pertinet, spectat inter occasum solis et Septentriones.*

3. J. Caesar., de Bello Gallico, lib. iii.

4. Id., lib. viii.

action: their defeat, of course, was the consequence; great numbers perished by the sword, and those who fled to the mountains fell victims to hunger. It is worthy of remark that, in this contest, the army of Agrippa was supplied with provisions by a fleet from Britain.

As the history of the Cantabri is so little known, it may, perhaps, not be thought irrelevant to insert a short extract from the account of the Cantabrian War, as related by Mariana, the Spanish historian. After describing the flourishing state of Spain in the early part of the age of Augustus, he says:

> In the height of this prosperity, when Spain flourished with riches and plenty, there broke out a new war, which proved more fierce and bloody than was imagined. This war was begun by the Cantabri, a fierce people, till then not entirely subdued by the Romans, as being the stubbornest nation of Spain, and protected by the harshness of the country they inhabited. Ptolemy says, the Cantabri bordered on the east upon the Antigones, on the west upon the Lungones, on the south they were bounded by the river Ebro, and on the north by the Cantabrian Sea, or Bay of Biscay. Their principal towns were Julioborga and Vellica. Others, and with reason, extend the bounds of Cantabria as far as the Pyrenean Mountains. At this time the Cantabri were a rude and fierce people, and had no use of gold or silver. The women, as well as the men, were of large stature; on their heads they wore a dress like a turban, and not unlike to what the women of Biscay now use. The women tilled the land, and when they were delivered of their children, the men themselves lay in, and they tended them, as is now used in certain parts of Brazil. In their dances they made a noise with their fingers and castanets. The men brought the portion when they married. They had

always poison prepared to kill themselves rather than suffer any violence. In order to commence the war, they stirred up the people of Asturias and Gallicia to take up arms, and that done, made incursions into the neighbouring country that was subject to the Romans. This did not only strike a terror into the natives, but perplexed the Emperor Augustus, fearing it might be the beginning of a more dangerous war than others expected. Augustus being come into Spain, forces resorted to him from all parts, so that he gathered a formidable army. They marched towards Biscay, and encamped near Segisama, supposed to be that now called Brisama, in Guipuscoa, betwixt Aspeitia and Tolosa. Then being divided into three parts, they soon subdued all the neighbouring country. The Cantabri, not trusting to their own strength, to avoid coming to a battle, withdrew with their goods and families unto the mountains, which prolonged the war, and made it be feared it would last long. Augustus, what with vexation, and what with the unwholesomeness of the air, fell sick, and was carried away to Tarragona. Caius Antistius, and Publius Firmius, were left to prosecute the war in Gallicia. Publius Carisius in Asturias. M. Agrippa was left with the supreme command. He was then the Emperor's favourite, and afterwards married his daughter Julia. Agrippa gathered a fleet from Britain, to furnish him with provisions, and at the same time to straiten the Cantabri by sea. Hunger pressing the Cantabri, they resolved to try the fortune of a battle, but being a rude people under no command, and without sense of honour, they were easily put to rout. Upon the coast of the ocean near to Segisama, rises the mountain Hirmius, by the Latins called Vinius, of difficult ascent, where many of them that fled saved themselves. The Romans, to avoid encountering with the strength of the place, and with men that were desperate, drew a trench quite round, and fortified it. So those miserable people were reduced to such extremity, they being obstinate not to surrender, and the Romans not to quit them, that the greatest part perished. A town near Brisama, then called Aracil, now Arraxil, after a long siege, was taken and destroyed by the Romans, Meanwhile while Antistius and Firmius were not idle in Gallicia, but drew a trench about the mountain Midulia, fifteen leagues in compass, where a great number of those people were retired, and after suffering the utmost extremities, (like the Cantabri,) part of them slew themselves with their swords, and others drank the poisonous juice of a tree that grows there. In Asturias, the war was carried on with the like success; for those people, thinking to surprise Carisius, who had divided his army into three parts, their design being discovered by the Tregenci, their confederates, were themselves oppressed by Carisius, who came upon them when they least expected it. Such as escaped fled to the city of Lancia, now Oviedo, where they fortified themselves, and held out a long siege, but were at last forced to surrender, and submit to the conqueror. Augustus, the war being ended, returned into Cantabria, where he pardoned the multitude; but, lest the roughness of the mountains might again encourage them to rebel, he caused them to come down and live in the plain country; and also to give a certain number of hostages. Many of the most obstinate were sold as slaves[1].

1. Stephen's Translation, chap. vii. lib. 3.

No sooner had Augustus returned to Rome, than the Cantabri again took up arms, and Agrippa, who had gone into Gaul, returned, and attacked them. The Cantabri were at first successful, but the Romans ultimately prevailed. It appears an incontrovertible fact, that though the Cantabrians do not now answer exactly to the description given of them by the Romans, yet they have retained their original language through all the different changes of government, to which their country has been subjected. Although in crossing the Pyrenean frontier we make a sudden transition from the character and language of Spain to that of France, yet, in the country here described, the great majority of the inhabitants still speak the ancient Cantabrian language, differing indeed in dialects in each of the provinces where it is spoken, but in all retaining the character of the original, known under the name of the Vaskian, Baskian, or, as it is called, the Basque or Bazque language. A number of words and phrases, it is true, have crept into their language during the occupation of Cantabria by foreign nations, and hence it has been inferred by some that the Cantabri were originally of the same stock with such foreigners; the fact, however, seems otherwise; and later inquiries have determined the point, that the language now spoken has, in reality, no connexion with the Bas Breton, Welsh, Erse, or other Celtic dialects.

Bouterwek, in the Introduction to his History of Spanish Literature, makes mention of the Cantabrian, Baskian, or Biscayan language, and says, that it was spoken by the greatest part of the inhabitants of Navarre, though the nobles spoke the Catalonian of Arragon, resembling the Provençal, but that the Cantabrian has no resemblance to the three great idioms spoken in the early part of the thirteenth century by the inhabitants of the three great kingdoms of the Peninsula. Many of the old commentators and historians have fallen into the error of confounding the Vaskian or Baskian with the Vasconian, spoken by the inhabitants to the southward of the Garonne; the latter is, however, a Latinized dialect, the Patois of Gascony, and has every appearance of being a remnant of the old Provençal.

The tract of country where the Basque language is spoken, is pretty accurately defined; and if due allowance be made for the rate of travelling in those days, the account of Scaliger will mark very nearly the extent of country occupied at the present day by the descendants of the ancient Cantabrians.

In the ingenious work of Adelung, (*Mithridates, oilier allgemeine Sprachenkunde*, published at Berlin in 1809,) there are many interesting particulars collected respecting the ancient territory, language, and manners of the Cantabrians or Basques; and, in the supplement to his work, more details are given by Wilhelm von Humboldt, who has added to his treatise a selection of words, arranged in alphabetical order, from the Basque Vocabulary.

After describing the ancient inhabitants of the tract of country between the Pyrenees and the Rhone, Adelung remarks:

> Yet all these people are vanished, and their language by degrees lost. Only there still exists a real Cantabrian remnant on both sides of the Pyrenees, in the present Spain and France, from the sea on the north as far as Pamplona; in the present Biscay, which Pliny knew under the name of Vascones. This people owe the preservation of their language and independence particularly to their residence in the mountains, where they were neither disturbed by the Romans nor Arabians. The Romans treated them as friends and allies, and as they did not place any colony amongst them, their language remained quite pure. The Arabi-

ans also let them alone, but not so the Visigoths, who established and supported many small states amongst them; and it may be owing to this circumstance that there are so many German words existing in their language. Hence the Basques believe that they have preserved the old Cantabrian Noblesse genuine and pure, and the lowest labourer holds himself, in point of nobility, upon a level with the wealthiest of the upper classes. The Spaniards call these people Bascongados, and the language Bascongada and Bascuence, the last from *ence* and *ante*, kind and manner, and *vasco*. By the French, the inhabitants are called Basques and Biscaines. They extend these names out farther, even to the Gascons, who have nothing in common with them, but quite the contrary, and are hated by them most vehemently. A Basque can bear any other affront offered him, but that of being called a Gascon; this he will either revenge himself, or carry his anger to the grave. They call themselves Escualdunac, and their language Escuara. Their language still exists on both sides of the Northern Pyrenees, partly in Spain, partly in France; in Spain, in the province of Biscay, and in the country of Guipuscoa and Alava, and in the kingdom of Upper Navarre; in France, in Lower Navarre, in the country of Labourt and Soule, which together are called Basque. It is only in the country, amongst the lowest classes, that it is spoken. Amongst the higher classes, and in towns, it is never made use of, but either French or Spanish is spoken.

The Basques have of late years maintained their ancient character as good soldiers, particularly for the service of light infantry. Horace makes frequent mention of them, and always as warlike, fierce, and unconquerable. They pride themselves much on their skill as marksmen. The character given of them by the biographer of the Duke D'Espernon, who has been before quoted, is by no means flattering. In describing the invasion of the Spaniards in 1636, he says:

> The Spanish council having determined to invade the kingdom in several places at once, principally hasted to enter into Guienne; to come to which province, they were to pass through the country of Labourt, (which is that of Biscaye) and by the way highly threatened the city of Bayonne. They knew very well the Duke of Espernon had no forces to send into that country; neither had he had them, durst he indeed have done it, without the consent of the inhabitants; lest, being a choleric, and impatient people, as they naturally are, any thing he should do of that kind, out of care to preserve them, should put them upon desperate resolutions, and make them wilfully lose themselves. They had, before they came, so despised the enemies' forces, that they would not endure any one should think of contributing to their preservation; a security that did not a little afflict the Duke, who had been of old acquainted with the humour of this people, and knew them to be as timorous and dejected, when any danger was near at hand, as they were stout and haughty when it was remote, and out of the prospect of their fear.

Entering among such a people, it was impossible not to feel an interest, as well as a desire to ascertain, how far their modern character had undergone a change, from their intervention between the two civilized nations of France and Spain. Unfortunately, the state of warfare prevented our seeing the inhabitants divested of the restraint imposed by so unsettled a condition; but still we saw enough to prove their dissimilitude both from the French and Spaniards. Although there is a manifest shade of Spanish character intermixed in those of the south side of the Pyrenees, and of French in those on the north, it is seen rather in particular localities, and along the great line of communication between the two countries, than generally spread throughout the Basque provinces. Adelung is quite mistaken in his assertion, that the Escuara, or Bascuence, is only spoken in the country among the lower classes. It is in reality the vernacular tongue of all classes; and, at St. Jean de Luz, was invariably spoken by the citizens among themselves; but, when they have occasion to address a stranger, or happen to be in mixed company of French or Spaniards, they speak French or Spanish, with which languages most of the townsmen are acquainted. During recent wars, the French government has always adopted the policy of appointing Basque generals to command the troops of that country, as they are with difficulty led by other commanders; and it is with great reluctance that they ever serve beyond the limits of their own territory.

In the present contest, when the allied troops first entered their territory, the great mass of the inhabitants, particularly those of the villages, were found to have retreated with the French army into the interior; but as soon as they began to discover that they had formed false notions of the English army, which, instead of maintaining itself at the expense of the conquered country, scrupulously paid for every article of provision; when they were told that private property was respected, they now sought every favourable opportunity of returning to their homes. It was said, and there is little doubt of the fact, that the French authorities strenuously endeavoured to dissuade the Basques from their intention of returning to their houses, but that their clamours at length prevailed, and they obtained permission to that effect; in, consequence of which, about three thousand of them returned to St. Jean de Luz, Urogne, and the surrounding country, before the end of November.

St. Jean de Luz had rather a gloomy appearance when the troops first went into cantonments; but now the shops were opened, and the town became a bustling scene of traffic for every article of supply required by the army. Provisions were, however, always dear, as the influx of so many strangers soon made away with the ordinary supply of the place, and the surplus was of course obliged to be obtained from great distances. Many Spaniards had set up shops in the town, and they were of great use in supplying provisions, and even luxuries, which their facilities of transport enabled them to bring from the adjoining provinces of Spain. Even the women, from the mountainous country around St. Andero, brought, in truck-baskets slung over their shoulders, butter, chocolate, honey, &c. The costume of these active pedestrians was very singular and gaudy. Notwithstanding the motley race who now were collected in this little town, perfect order was preserved. The Allies felt the beneficial effects of the Marquess of Wellington's having rigidly enforced the protection of private property; for, instead of meeting with a race of hostile inhabitants, on whom the French government relied for commencing a harassing partisan warfare, nothing could exceed the harmony which prevailed between the Basques and the troops who were now spread over their country. Their confidence daily increasing, about three thousand more of the natives passed the line of allied outposts, on the 3rd of December, and came back to their different villages. Many young men were amongst these, disguised as women, to avoid being detained by the French authorities for the new conscription. Their fears were ludicrous when detected in this disguise, apprehending that they would be sent back to Bayonne, or be treated as spies. Yet it was repeatedly announced in the *Moniteur*, that the Basques had risen en masse; and that the whole population, from eighteen to forty-five years of age, had taken up arms, leaving none in the mountains but old men, women, and children; and that they were perpetually harassing the English at every point, not allowing them a moment of repose; which is just about as true as, another article in the same paper, which asserts, that in the combats which had taken place between the 9th and the 13th of December, the allied army had lost fifteen thousand men, whilst the losses of the French did not amount to one-fourth part: that the uttermost consternation prevailed in the army of Lord Wellington; and that, with the dissensions among the Allies, the desertions that took place, the disease and privations which the army was suffering, and the numerous shipwrecks on the coast, which served to feed the French army, the position of the English became, from day to day, more critical. These and similar falsehoods were repeated, from time to time, in the official gazette; but not a word of the capture of St. Sebastian by storm, of the surrender of Pamplona, of the crossing of the Bidassoa, and the establishment of the allied army on the French territory. Of these circumstances it was attempted, by the usual system of falsehood and delusion, to keep the people of France in profound ignorance; but the friends of the Bourbons were in the secret, and quietly taking their measures to avail themselves of the catastrophe, which it was now evident was about to close the career of Napoleon.

In the meantime, the best spirit and the most cordial unanimity prevailed among the officers and troops of the allied army. The state of the weather allowed them a little breathing time in their cantonments; and the officers were not idle in examining the neighbouring country.

The little port of Socoa, at the mouth of the bay of St. Jean de Luz, became an *entrepôt* for supplies of corn and biscuit, which was conveyed from thence to the different divisions of the army by large convoys of Spanish muleteers. The name of Socoa is from the Basque, Zocoa, which signifies an angular point or corner, the situation of Socoa being at the angular point of rock which terminates the Bay of St. Jean de Luz on its south-west side. Its little harbour is strongly fortified, and its batteries serve at the same time to guard the entrance to the bay. A beautiful martello-tower crowns the defences, and commands the approaches to it for a considerable extent. Fort Socoa, with its martello-tower, forms a very pleasing object in the view from St. Jean de Luz; but the most striking view of it is from the heights terminating the point of land with which the fort is connected; from thence we have complete command of the harbour and the handsome stone piers which enclose it. In this view, the little fort and pier of Ste. Barbe are seen on the opposite side of the bay, and the distance terminates in the low range of hilly ground towards Bidart and Bayonne.

Chapter 5

The Defeat of Marshal Soult

With the commencement of December, the weather once more became more favourable for active operations. Though a considerable fall of snow had taken place on the upper regions of the Pyrenees, the lower parts of the mountains remained quite clear, and in the plains and valleys the weather might be considered as mild. The Marquess of Wellington now determined to avail himself of the improved state of the roads and of the fall of the rivers (as sudden as their rise in this mountainous country), to establish the right wing of the allied army upon the right bank of the Nive, and in a position which would intercept the direct communication between Bayonne and St. Jean Pied de Port. It had been the Field-Marshal's intention to cross the Nive in following up the victory gained over the French in November, but the heavy, and almost incessant, rains, put a stop to farther progress at that time. The enemy, in the mean while, guarded with his left wing the right bank of the Nive, and communicated by strong patrols of cavalry, with a division of his army, under General Paris, stationed at St. Jean Pied de Port.

The 9th of December was the day fixed on for carrying into effect the Field-Marshal's intention; which he resolved to delay no longer, although heavy rain again fell on the preceding day. The first and fifth divisions, with Lord Aylmer's brigade, forming together the left wing of the army under Sir John Hope, were ordered to advance by the great road leading from St. Jean de Luz towards Bayonne to reconnoitre the enemy's entrenched camp opposite the village of Anglet; and to examine the course of the Adour, from the flank of the entrenched camp, resting on that river opposite the old convent of St. Bernard, to the sea. Major-General Alten was directed to reconnoitre, with the light division, the entrenched camp between the right of Sir John Hope's corps and the left bank of the Nive, by advancing from Bassussarry along the road leading from St. Pé towards Bayonne. This operation, by menacing the enemy's camp on the most important side, was calculated to withdraw his immediate attention from that part of his army which occupied the right bank of the Nive, against which the principal efforts of the British Field-Marshal were intended to be directed.

To dislodge the French from the banks of the Nive, Marshal Beresford was directed to effect the passage of that river with the sixth division opposite Ustaritz, whilst Sir Rowland Hill should make his passage at Cambo with the second division. Major-General Pringle's brigade of the second division, forming an intermediate corps between those under Marshal Beresford and Sir Rowland Hill, was directed to cross at the ford of Halsou, a village about midway between Ustaritz and Cambo, but upon the right bank of the Nive. In the town of St. Jean de Luz there had been no indication of the approaching movement, till a convoy of some pontoon boats, a few days before, created a suspicion of approaching operations.

On the 7th of December, intelligence was brought to the army, of the great overthrow which the French had sustained in the battle of Hanau, of the important event of the restoration of Hanover to the British crown, and of the declaration of independence and exemption from French bondage, made by the States of Holland. The receipt of this intelligence was well calculated to inspire animation into the breasts of our allies, who began now to look forward with a degree of hope they had hardly before ventured to indulge, of the speedy overthrow of the tyranny of Buonaparte. Even the French people themselves appeared to rejoice at the news, as affording to them the prospect of a release from the calamities of war. We could not but observe with what astonishment and apparent delight they gazed upon Captain Mitchell's excellent brigade of artillery, as it passed through St. Jean de Luz, towards the outposts of Sir John Hope's corps.

Early on the morning of the 8th, a distant cannonade was heard in the direction of our right wing, but it was of short duration, and nothing of consequence occurred. In the afternoon of this day, we first heard of the intended movement on the morrow, and immediately put ourselves in readiness for a fresh advance. Accordingly, at one o'clock in the morning, the drums beat to arms, and in an hour after, the first and second brigades of Guards assembled on their respective parades, in St. Jean de Luz and Ciboure. At three o'clock the brigades commenced their march along the great road which leads to Bayonne. It was a wet morning, and the roads being very bad, the march was excessively fatiguing to the men. On arriving at the Plateau of Barouillet, in advance of Bidart, the brigades halted till the whole of the first division, under Major-General Howard, was assembled. At dawn of day it ceased raining, and soon after we discovered the fifth division, under Major-General Hay, supported by the 12th Light Dragoons; crossing the valley which separates the hilly ground of Biarits from that of Bidart; its left extending to the sea-coast, and its right in communication with the first division. Both divisions were in columns of battalions. The light German brigade was sent out in advance of the right of the first division, *en tirailleur*. The light companies of the fifth division formed a cordon in front of that part of the line, whilst the light companies of the brigades of Guards and the King's German Legion, line battalions, covered the front of the first division, along the great road leading between the Etang de Chuhigue on its left, and the Etang de Rousta on its right.

At eight o'clock the first shot was fired; and immediately the whole line of light troops commenced a most spirited fire on those of the enemy, who tenaciously contested every hedge and bank that afforded shelter from our fire, and from whence they could take deliberate aim at our men. The artillery posted themselves on the eminences along the whole line, and by a fire of shells greatly aided in dislodging the French *tirailleurs* from behind the hedges and banks. The whole line made gradual progress in advance, the enemy not venturing to risk the approach of the allied columns, but retreating before them to Anglet. At one o'clock in the afternoon, the first division gained the heights on the right of the Bayonne road, opposite to Anglet, the light infantry driving the enemy down the slopes to the entrenched camp. The fifth division had made equal progress on the left, sweeping the whole country between Anglet and the sea, as far as the banks of the Adour, and occupying with its light infantry the Bois de Bayonne, a large pine-wood, which covers the whole space on the left of the Adour, between the entrenched camp and the sea.

Whilst the left wing, under General Sir John Hope, executed the movements on the left, the light division, under General Alten, made a corresponding advance between the left wing and the banks of the Nive; gallantly driving the enemy from behind a deep morass, which covered his advanced posts in front of Bassussarry, and compelling the French to retreat to the entrenched camp, near the Château de Marrac, the place in which King Ferdinand was so perfidiously betrayed by Napoleon.

At day-break Marshal Beresford crossed the Nive at Ustaritz, whilst Sir Rowland Hill attacked the enemy behind the Nive opposite Cambo. On every point the operations went on successfully. The sixth division, having made rapid progress towards the road leading from St. Jean Pied de Port to Bayonne, menaced the rear of part of the French left wing, compelling them to make a long detour to rejoin their comrades on the hills about Petit Monguerre. In this manner the allied army formed a sort of crescent which straitened the enemy in his positions before Bayonne.

It had been previously arranged, that the left wing should retire to its old position as soon as the right wing had accomplished its object; and it was to commence retiring at six o'clock in the evening, unless a countermand should arrive. In the afternoon the rain fell again very heavily; and it was with some difficulty that the troops got their bivouac-fires lighted, the men supposing that they were to remain on the ground which they had gained. The weather, however, was much too bad to admit the possibility of the soldiers remaining any length of time in such exposed situations; and as, at six o'clock, no counter-order had arrived, the troops of the left wing began their march back to St. Jean de Luz, and towards their several cantonments; the fifth division forming the rear guard to the whole. It was quite dark when the brigades began to retire, and the rain fell in torrents; and, on again entering the main road, it was found that the passage of the artillery, and the advance of so many troops along it, had so completely broken it up, and it was besides so deluged with rain, that, in some of the hollow-ways, it was knee deep of mud. Some idea may be formed of the difficulty of marching troops along this road when it is stated, that a little drummer, belonging to the third battalion of the First Guards, literally stuck fast in the mud, and was obliged to be lifted out, and carried for some distance by a couple of soldiers. The distance from St. Jean de Luz to the entrenched camp of Bayonne, is about twelve miles; and, as the men were marching nearly the whole day, the fatigued state and the muddy condition in which the brigades arrived late at night, in St. Jean de Luz, will readily be imagined. They had been on foot little short of twenty-four hours; and many of them were so completely exhausted, as to sink down powerless by the road-side; the weather continuing nearly the whole night as bad as it well could be. The light division also was withdrawn to its old cantonment, about Arcangues and Bassussarry.

At dawn of day, on the 10th, the enemy, in his turn, moved out of Bayonne with a strong corps, and attacked the fifth division, which had occupied its old station at Barouillet, in advance of the left wing; attacking at the same time the light division at Arcangues. The Portuguese brigade, commanded by General Campbell, was stationed on the great Bayonne road in front of the fifth division, which occupied the plateau of Barouillet. Major-General Robinson's brigade supported the Portuguese. To the right of Barouillet, the first brigade of the fifth division, commanded by Colonel Greville, guarded the approach to the Bayonne road from the side of, the plateau of Bassussarry. Between this point and the light division at Arcangues, there was a broad-valley left almost without defence by the Allies, as it appeared certain that the French commander would not attempt advancing through this interval as long as the Allies maintained the positions of Barouillet and Arcangues.

The enemy advanced in two strong columns, the first composed of several battalions, by the great road from Bayonne; attacking, early in the morning, the outposts of the fifth division, and driving them back upon their supports on the Plateau of Barouillet. The second came forward by the Plateau of Bassussarry, throwing out a strong line of *tirailleurs* supported by battalions, against the light division, which had entrenched itself in the village of Arcangues. The main body, however, pushed forward a short way beyond the left flank of the light division, sending forward strong columns to attack the right of the fifth division, thus manifesting his intention of penetrating towards Arbonne, between and in rear of the two divisions. Sir John Hope, accompanied by his staff, was ever in the thickest of the fight, encouraging by his personal example the troops of the fifth division, which had to sustain severe attacks on both flanks, and which seemed on the point of being overpowered by the formidable numbers of the enemy. The Portuguese, supported by Major-General Robinson's brigade, sustained the attack from the great road in the most gallant style; but their exposed situation made them suffer considerable loss, and Major-General Robinson was wounded. There is a thick coppice-wood in front of Barouillet; and to the right of the great Bayonne road, it is separated from the Maison de Barouillet, by a large field and an orchard. The enemy advanced through the wood and orchard against Barouillet, when the Portuguese on the left flank, and the ninth foot on the right, wheeled round and attacked the rear of the French columns; this bold manoeuvre defeated the enemy's project at that point, and some hundred prisoners were taken. It was about mid-day when the brigades of Guards were ordered to march from St. Jean de Luz, to support the fifth division. They arrived at the Plateau of Barouillet about three o'clock in the afternoon, just as the enemy had been checked in his attempt to dislodge the fifth division. The sight of fresh troops coming into the field cast a damp on the ardour of the enemy, and the firing gradually ceased with the close of evening. The attack upon the light division at Arcangues was most animated. Again and again the French tried to dislodge the brave light division from the defences of the church-yard and château; they were always repulsed with great loss. The French troops, however, retained possession, during the night, of the Plateau of Bassussarry, which joins the Plateau of Barouillet in front of the mayor's house. The object of Marshal Soult's attack was, doubtless, to oblige the left wing to retreat upon St. Jean de Luz, and thus cause the troops under Sir Rowland Hill, who had crossed the Nive, to make a corresponding retrograde movement, and thus again enable himself to have direct communication with St. Jean Pied de Port.

Meantime Sir Rowland Hill, finding on the morning of the 10th that the enemy had withdrawn the main part of his forces from the heights of Monguerre, advanced to that position, establishing his right upon the left bank of the Adour; his centre upon the heights in front of Vieux Monguerre; and his left upon the Nive, opposite Villefranque, where a pontoon bridge was laid down, to keep up communication with the centre of the army. The sixth division re-crossed to the left bank of the Nive.

A glance at the plan will immediately explain the great advantage the enemy had over the Allies, in the facility with which he could execute his movements. Bayonne might be considered as the centre of a circle; in the circumference of which the Allies were posted, having their communications divided by the Nive, and the worst possible cross roads to march on, in case of support being required, either upon one flank or the other. The facilities which the enemy now possessed of making separate attacks, direct upon any part of the Marquess of Wellington's army, are obvious. These he could execute without any risk to his rear or flanks, as the entrenched camp before Bayonne was a sufficient safeguard against whichever wing of the Allies he might choose to leave unmolested. In this manner he was able to paralyse a large portion of the allied army, by merely leaving just a sufficiency of troops to guard his entrenched camp. How much more then is it to the credit of the Allies, who, by single divisions, defeated the strong columns which the enemy had sent forward to the attack.

The first division occupied Bidart during the night, between the 10th and 11th, to be in readiness to support the fifth division in the event of a renewed attack on the following morning. But the enemy withdrew his troops to the heights behind the Etang de Chuhigue and the Etang de Rousta, during the night, leaving strong picquets upon the Plateau of Bassussarry, and on its continuation in front of Barouillet.

On the morning of the 11th, at dawn, the light troops of the fifth division drove in the enemy's picquets, and the most advanced sentries were again pushed forward to their old line. The rain had fallen the greater part of the preceding day, and the troops began to experience the harassing effects of being constantly on the alert, upon ground which was soon trampled into mud. Nothing material happened during the forenoon; the men received their rations, and parties were sent out unarmed to cut wood for cooking. The weather brightened, and all was tranquil on the outposts. About two o'clock, however, some stir was visible in the enemy's line, and in some places the French were seen cutting gaps in the fences for the passage of their artillery; a few moments after, they commenced a furious attack along the great Bayonne road, driving in the picquets upon their supports. The hill in front of Barouillet again became the scene of a hard contest. There was a general shout of "to arms" the moment this attack commenced; and the soldiers, who had gone in front of Barouillet to cut wood, ran back in all haste to get themselves armed and accoutred. The French, seeing a number of men running to the rear, imagined that the Allies had taken a panic, and set up loud cheers of *"En avant, en avant!"* In a few moments, however, the whole left wing was formed in perfect order. The fifth division, part of Lord Aylmer's brigade, and the Portuguese, in first line, having its left resting on the Etang de Chuhigue, and extending from thence to the right, across the wood and orchard before mentioned, in front of Barouillet; the right resting upon the edge of the valley, between the Plateau of Barouillet and Arcangues. The brigades of Guards, and part of Lord Aylmer's brigade, were in columns of companies, and formed a second line, in rear of Barouillet, on a narrow ridge of heathy ground. The Portuguese brigades attached to the first and fifth divisions again behaved most gallantly in sustaining the enemy's onset, and the fifth division again maintained possession of the line in front of the mayor's house. The French made a feint attack upon Arcangues, to cover a more serious movement against the fifth division, along the Plateau of Bassussarry. Sir John Hope showed as before the same glorious example of heroism, in exposing his person wherever the enemy's efforts seemed most formidable; and it is wonderful that himself and his staff, who were, during the whole of these attacks, exposed to the hottest fire, escaped with so little injury. The Marquess of Wellington had ordered the picquets to be withdrawn from the hill in front, in the event of being attacked, but directed the line of position in front of Barouillet to be strictly maintained; and night once more put an end to the contest, leaving the opposite armies in the same positions as on the former night; all Marshal Soult's efforts to drive back the left wing proving ineffectual.

As soon as it was sufficiently dark to prevent any change of position which might be made by our troops from being discernible by the enemy, the first division, under Major-General Howard, relieved the fifth division, the latter forming in second line, on the same ground that the first had occupied. The two brigades of Guards occupied the line in front of Barouillet. The second brigade, consisting of the Coldstream and Third Guards, under Major-General Stopford, were on the left, in front of the mayor's house. The first brigade, consisting of the first and third battalions of the First Guards, under Colonel Maitland, were to the right of the second brigade, on the brow of a hill, separated by a narrow ravine from the height so often contested, and of which the enemy retained possession at night-fall. At this point there is a small farm-house, and the slope of the hill down into the ravine in front is skirted by a remarkably thick coppice-wood; here the picquets of the third battalion were posted. On the right of this house there is another large orchard, which was occupied by the picquets of the first battalion, formed on the high ground a little in rear, under the command of Colonel Askew. The third battalion, under the Hon. Colonel Stuart, was on its left, in rear of the little farm-house just mentioned; a piquet of light infantry, commanded by Captain Lord Saltoun, was stationed at a hut in the wood, upon the left of the first brigade, to keep up communication with Major-General Stopford's brigade, and guard against any attack along a cross road, which leads from the height occupied by the enemy, to the farm of Barouillet. Lieutenant-Colonel West commanded the picquets of light infantry guarding the extreme right.

With the close of day the rain again began to fall, and the night was so dark that it was difficult to avoid interfering with the enemy's picquets, when posting the sentries at the bottom of the ravine. Towards morning the weather became more settled, and at sunrise it was beautifully clear. We could now distinguish the heads of the French columns on the ridge opposite to our position. Staff-officers were seen riding about in all directions, and the French drums and trumpets were heard to sound at intervals along their line. There was every appearance of the main body of the enemy being assembled at this point; and it was supposed that it was about to make a fresh attack against the left wing. Much precaution was observed in posting the picquets in the most favourable situations, and in placing strong supports immediately in rear; for this part of the line was lower than that occupied by the enemy, whose position, therefore, in some degree commanded that of the Guards.

The brave Sir Edward Packenham came up to the picquets, and gave some directions to the officers on duty there. About ten o'clock, a strong line of *tirailleurs* advanced from the crest of the enemy's position, along the brow of the ravine, in front of the first brigade of Guards. Some artillery had been stationed at the farm-house before described, and on seeing this body of *tirailleurs*, the officer in command of the guns, imagining that the attack was about to commence, fired at them, and in a moment after the whole line of picquets commenced a hot fire, which was kept up on both sides with great warmth. But no considerable body of the enemy made any advance, and it seemed probable that Marshal Soult, on finding the Allies so fully prepared for an attack, desisted from his intention of trying to force back the left wing.

The Marquess of Wellington had foreseen the enemy's intentions, and moved the fourth and seventh divisions to the rear of the line occupied by the light division at Arcangues, and that occupied by Major-General Howard, in readiness to afford support, in case of need, at either point, prior to the attack on the 11th. The readiness with which the Field-Marshal foresaw, and provided against Marshal Soult's manoeuvres, made the enemy's advantageous position of little real benefit to him. The skirmish was kept up during a great part of the day, and some brave officers and men were killed, and many wounded. The firing opposite the brigade of Major-General Stopford was also briskly kept up during the whole time. Captain Watson, the Adjutant to the Third Guards, was one of the first who fell; he had early in the morning remarked what abundance of laurel grew around the house of Barouillet, to deck the graves of those who should die on the field of glory; and fate struck him off the first. Lieutenant-Colonel Martin, commanding the piquet of the first battalion of the First Guards, was shot whilst giving some directions to those around him in the orchard where his men were stationed; and almost immediately after, Captain Thomson, an officer of the highest promise; also in the first battalion, fell in the act of directing the fire of his men against the French *tirailleurs*. Several officers were wounded; the total number, however, of killed and wounded in both brigades was below two hundred.

The tenacity with which the left wing of the army maintained its position, apparently convinced the enemy of the impracticability of gaining his object on that side; but conceiving that the Marquess of Wellington's attention must now be almost wholly occupied in securing the defence of the left wing, he withdrew the great body of his army within the entrenched camp of Bayonne, leaving merely a cordon of outposts in front of Sir John Hope's corps, during the night. But Lord Wellington penetrated the enemy's design, and made immediate preparations to support the troops under Sir Row land Hill;

rightly judging that Marshal Soult's next efforts would be on that side. The fourth and sixth divisions, with the greater part of the third, were moved to the banks of the Nive, to be in readiness to support those between that river and the Adour. Marshal Beresford crossed over with the sixth division, early in the morning of the 13th. Sir Rowland Hill, having ascertained that the French army was assembling, during the night of the 12th, in great force, opposite to his position, made preparations for receiving his meditated attack. He distributed his corps in the following order: — upon the left, in front of the village of Villefranque, there is a long ridge of hilly ground, extending from that village towards Bayonne, bounded on one hand by the Nive, and on the other by large mill-dams, in a deep hollow, which separates the ridge from the heights of Monguerre. Upon this ridge the twenty-eighth, thirty-fourth, and thirty-ninth regiments were stationed, forming Major-General Pringle's brigade of the second division. Upon the right, in front of the village of Vieux Monguerre, there is also a long ridge of hill, bounded on the right by the Adour, and upon the left by mill-dams, which separate it from the heights in the centre, in the same manner as the heights of Villefranque are bounded. Upon this spot the third, thirty-first, fifty-seventh, and sixty-eighth regiments were stationed, forming Major-General Byng's brigade of the second division. The centre ridge of heights, opposite the village of Saint Pierre, was at first occupied by Brigadier-General Ashworth's Portuguese brigade, consisting of the sixth and eighteenth line, and sixth Caçadores. But as soon as the enemy's attack was manifested against the centre, the brigade of Major-General Barnes, also belonging to the second division, was brought forward from the heights of Petit Monguerre, and took its station on the right of General Ashworth's

Portuguese. The general form of the line thus occupied was that of a crescent, and the enemy's attacks were principally directed against the centre of the concave side. The extent of ground taken up was about four English miles, from the Adour on the right to the Nive on the left.

In this manner, the second division, under the command of Lieutenant-General the Honourable Sir William Stewart, waited the approach of the enemy.

Soon after eight o'clock the out-posts, on the great road leading from St. Jean Pied de Port, through St. Pierre to Bayonne, were briskly attacked by overwhelming numbers of *tirailleurs*, and the French columns advanced close in, the rear, up the long slopes in front of the centre position, the enemy's column extending a good way on both sides of the road. A large body, at the same time, advanced against the left of the centre, up the hollow way which separated it, from Major-General' Pringle's brigade on the left, the right of the French columns resting upon the mill-dams. As there was no longer any doubt of the enemy's intention to pierce the centre, Sir Rowland Hill directed the whole of Major-General Byng's brigade, excepting the third regiment and light companies of the others, to move to their left, and support the right of the centre. Brigadier-General Buchan's Portuguese brigade was moved up from behindVillefranque to support the left of the centre. Lieutenant-Colonel Ross's troop of horse-artillery, and Lieutenant-Colonel Tullock's' Portuguese brigade of guns, had also been moved up in aid of the centre, and a most destructive fire was opened against the French columns in their advance; the havoc caused by their fire on the great road was terrific. The light companies of General Barnes's brigade, commanded by Major Gordon of the fiftieth regiment, which had gone forward in support of the picquets, were borne back by the massy columns of the enemy upon the main line, the light troops bravely contesting every step of the ground; and the enemy, under a tremendous fire, succeeded in establishing himself upon a height close to the position; and here a long and obstinate conflict was kept up, Major-General Barnes's brigade and the eighteenth regiment of line in General Ashworth's Portuguese, repeatedly dislodging the enemy from this post, but he as often retook it; till Major-General Barnes, with the ninety-second Highlanders, commanded by Lieutenant-Colonel Cameron, supported on the left by the Portuguese, made a most gallant charge, and drove the enemy down from the position.

The sixth line and sixth Caçadores, upon the left centre, sustained a very formidable attack from the columns which had advanced up the hollow-way. The seventy-first regiment and a part of the ninety-second were sent to aid the Portuguese, but even this reinforcement was unable to prevent the enemy from gaining possession of a part of the position. Most fortunately, Brigadier-General Da Costa's brigade, consisting of the second and fourteenth Portuguese regiments of the line, in Major-General Le Cor's division, arrived at this critical moment and Sir William Stewart immediately directed the former regiment to turn the right flank of the attacking columns, whilst the fourteenth regiment, headed by its gallant commander, Major Pravassos, attacked the enemy in front, charging in columns over the rugged ground between his troops and those of the enemy, when he instantly attacked with the bayonet. The French columns were immediately checked, and the brave Portuguese, following up this success, killed great numbers of them. This gallant attack restored order upon the left of the centre.

The attack against Major-General Pringle was not so formidable; but a hot fire of *tirailleurs* was kept up to occupy the attention of his brigade, and prevent its aiding the troops in the centre. The Major-General, however, by judiciously placing his artillery on eminences that commanded the flank of the enemy's movements against the centre, and occupying a line at right angles to their's, contributed greatly to harass the French in their advance. In this position the twenty-eighth regiment caused the enemy considerable loss, by a well-directed flanking fire.

When Major-General Byng moved to the support of the centre, a whole French division crossed the mill-stream between St. Pierre and Vieux Monguerre, and made a vigorous attack against the third regiment and light troops, commanded by Colonel Bunbury. The enemy at first succeeded in gaining possession of the height and village of Vieux Monguerre; but, on being directed by Sir Rowland Hill to recover the post, the Buffs and light infantry gallantly drove the enemy back, although greatly superior in numbers. The light companies, commanded by Captain Cameron of the third regiment, distinguished themselves in this attack, taking a field officer and a number of men prisoners.

The enemy had in this manner been defeated upon all points, suffering immense loss in every attack. The great superiority of numbers brought forward by Marshal Soult required the utmost ability of Sir Rowland Hill to prepare for his attacks, and the greatest gallantry and judgment in Sir William Stewart, and the brave generals acting under his orders, to repel them.

The next object was to dislodge the enemy from the ground in front of the entrenched camp, where he still remained in great force; and the French officers were observed to use ineffectual efforts to make their infantry again come forward to the attack, a warm cannonade being kept up during the whole time against the centre of the Allies. Sir William Stewart directed Major-General Byng to unite his brigade, and attack the French upon the opposite bank of the mill-stream, in front of the heights of

Vieux Monguerre. Major-General Byng attacked the enemy in the most gallant style, himself carrying the colours of the sixty-sixth (Provisional Battalion), and planting them on the hill forming the enemy's position, under a hot fire of musketry and artillery. The third regiment crossed the mill-stream in front of Vieux Monguerre, and co-operated in the attack of the hill. The brigade, thus united, succeeded in driving down the enemy within the suburb of St. Pierre. Soon after Brigadier-General Buchan's Portuguese brigade arrived, to support Major-General Byng. The French made an attempt to recover this point, but were repulsed. The ninth Caçadores, under Lieutenant-Colonel Browne, of Brigadier-General Buchan's Portuguese brigade, aided in the final repulse of the enemy. The third and sixth divisions arrived, in the latter part of the day, to support the corps of Sir Rowland Hill; but the victory was decided by the brave second division, commanded by General Stewart, aided by the Portuguese.

This brilliant victory closed the harassing service which the army had undergone during five successive days, and convinced the enemy of the invincible superiority of the Allies, and of the hopelessness of every effort to regain his lost ground. At night, the French army retreated within the entrenched camp between the Nive and Adour; and Sir Rowland Hill established his advanced posts on the verge of a ravine which guards its front, opposite to the village of St. Pierre.

The Marquess of Wellington had thus fully accomplished the object of defeating the enemy's manoeuvres, of cutting off his direct communication with St. Jean Pied de Port, and of confining him to the defence of his entrenched camp before Bayonne. St. Jean Pied de Port was observed by General Morillo's Spanish division during these operations. The allied troops were now in possession of a large tract of country, from whence they obtained a great part of their forage, obliging the enemy to draw his chief supplies from the country on the right bank of the Adour. The right wing, by its position on the left of the Adour, commanded the navigation of that river, and was often enabled to intercept the supplies destined for the French army. The roads on its right bank are generally so bad in the depth of winter, that the chief part of the provisions, for the support of the inhabitants of Bayonne, are brought in boats down the river. The positions likewise, now occupied by the army, were much more favourable for the prosecution of the campaign in the interior of the country, whenever a more favourable state of the weather should enable the Marquess to resume his operations.

These important results, however, cost the lives of a great number of brave officers and soldiers, besides a long list of wounded, including many most distinguished generals. In the battle of the 13th, Major-General Barnes, Lieutenant-General Le Cor, and Brigadier-General Ashworth, and nearly the whole of the staff and aides-de-camp of Sir William Stewart, General Barnes, and General Byng, were wounded. The fiftieth and ninety-second regiments suffered severely, losing many officers in killed and wounded. The total loss of the British, in the actions of the 9th, 10th, 11th, 12th, and 13th of December, amounted to one hundred and sixty-nine officers, and two thousand five hundred and sixteen sergeants, drummers, and privates, killed, wounded, and missing. That of the Portuguese amounted to one hundred and thirty-three officers, and two thousand two hundred and eleven sergeants, drummers, and privates, killed, wounded, and missing; making together a total of three hundred and two officers (including four generals,) and four thousand seven hundred and twenty-seven sergeants and privates, put hors de combat; and not fifteen thousand, as Marshal Soult is said to have reported, and as is stated in the Moniteur.

But if the loss of the Allies was severe, that of the enemy was much more so. In the battle of the 13th, which lasted from morning till night, the ground was covered with their slain; and it has been estimated that their total loss amounted to considerably more than six thousand men; though in the whole of the five days' fighting, the Moniteur, according to the Marshal's report, makes the loss sustained under four thousand men. Besides the serious losses of the enemy, Soult had the additional mortification of losing the two regiments of Frankfort and Nassau Usingen, who, on hearing that their countrymen had abjured the French yoke, came over, after the action of the 10th, to the outposts of the fourth division, in the centre of the allied army.

Tranquillity being again restored, the first division was marched back to its old cantonments; but to guard against surprise, and to give timely notice to the troops in their cantonments of any attack made by the enemy, telegraphic signal stations were formed at the churches of Guethary, Arcangues, and Vieux Monguerre. These communicated with a signal station upon a high sand-hill, on the north side of St. Jean de Luz, near the entrance to the town from the Bayonne-road. By an ingenious combination of flags, and barrels suspended from high signal-posts, it was found that notice could be almost instantaneously given at head-quarters, (now again established in St. Jean de Luz,) of whatever movement the enemy might undertake whether against the advanced posts of the left wing at Barouillet, the centre at Arcangues, or the right wing under Sir Rowland Hill between the Nive and Adour. To save time, the telegraphic sentences were so arranged, that each separate signal would at once explain the nature of the communication it was meant to convey.

CHAPTER 6
The Adour

The establishment of telegraphic signal stations, to give speedy notice of the enemy's movements, enabled the Marquess of Wellington to place once more the greater part of his army in cantonments; a point of most essential importance to the health of the troops, the maintenance of which required every exertion and care during the wet and cold weather, towards the close of the year. To make the duty at the outposts as light as possible, it was taken alternately by the different brigades in each division, the remainder returning to their cantonments in the intervals.

Marshal Soult had, on the failure of his efforts to drive back the right wing of the Allies from its position between the Nive and the Adour, withdrawn his right wing within the entrenched camp, which covered the approach to Bayonne on the side opposite to Anglet; retaining, however, that village, and the range of heights from Biarits to the Nive, with his out-picquets. The entrenched camp on this side rested its left flank on the Nive, below the Château de Marrac, and included that building and the walled gardens about it in its sweep, extending in the form of the segment of a circle, of which the cathedral of Bayonne may be considered as the centre, to the Adour, opposite to the Verrerie de St. Bernard, formerly a convent.

The situation of this camp is naturally marked out by a gentle rise in the ground along its whole front, of sufficient elevation, however, to command the country for more than a mile. The whole of this position was defended by a remarkably strong chain of entrenchments and redoubts, mounted with a formidable artillery. In many places the works included within their line the villas, or country-houses, of the neighbouring gentry, of which there are great numbers on all sides of Bayonne. These houses were loop-holed and fortified in such a manner, as to render each of them a petty fortress. The whole front was farther protected by a broad and deep morass, capable of being inundated at pleasure by sluices purposely constructed in the embankment, on the left of the Adour, at the point where the right flank of the camp rested on that river, which, at high water, rises considerably above the level of the morass. This morass was only passable on two points; the first, where the great road from St. Jean de Luz leads into Bayonne, opposite to Anglet; the second, where a natural rise of the ground connects the height of the entrenched camp near Marrac, with the tongue of land extending from Bassussarry, and forming the left bank of the Nive at this part. Both these points were guarded by the strongest redoubts; and the road from St. Jean de Luz was, in addition, protected by a strongly-fortified height, in advance of the entrenched camp, and separated from the sloping ground in front of Anglet by another morass, uniting with the former just below this point.

A similar chain of defences covered the approach to Bayonne, between the Nive and the Adour; and the whole range of these works was under cover of the guns on the fortifications of the city.

A camp so formed might well be deemed nearly impregnable. Marshal Soult, therefore, trusting in this secure *point-d'appui*, extended his line along the right bank of the

Adour, as far as the confluence of the Bidouze with it, just below Guiche. With the left wing-of his army, under General Clausel, he occupied the right bank of the Bidouze, and established his own head-quarters at Peyrehorade, a town situated at the junction of the Gave de Pau with the Gave d'Oleron, five miles above the point where the united stream flows into the Adour. The patrols of General Clausel's corps crossed to the left bank of the Bidouze, to observe the movements of the foraging parties of the Allies between that river and the Joyeuse, another small stream flowing into the Adour across that part of the country which lies between the Bidouze and the Nive. The extreme left of the enemy's line occupied St. Palais, from whence he was again enabled to hold communication with St. Jean Pied de Port, where Genera Harispe was stationed with a strong division, consisting partly of troops of the line and partly of National Guards. In front of the French left wing a division of Cavalry, under General Soult, (brother of the Marshal,) patrolled the country in the direction of Bouloc and Hasparren.

The enemy's army in this manner occupied an unusually extended circuit, doubling in the rear of the allied right wing. The month of December (1813) closed, however, without any occurrence of importance; but the new year had scarcely commenced, when active operations were renewed.

The Marquess of Wellington had placed Sir Thomas Picton's division in a position where he could observe the advanced posts of the enemy between St. Palais and Hasparren; and the Portuguese brigade of General Buchan on the left bank of the Joyeuse, and in La Bastide on its right bank, to guard the rear of his right wing. Information having been received at head-quarters, that the corps of General Clausel was assembling in force opposite these points, an alert took place along the whole line of the allied positions.

The troops under Clausel attacked and dislodged Major-General Buchan's brigade from its position at La Bastide on the Joyeuse, and established themselves on the heights of La Coste on its left bank. On the 3d of January, and on Tuesday the 4th, the drums beat to arms early in the morning at St. Jean de Luz. The brigades of Guards marched immediately to the outposts at Barouillet, where they took up the alignment of the whole left wing, in concert with the brigades of the King's German Legion; relieving, in this manner, the fifth division, which moved off to some ground farther to the right. A succession of reliefs took place along the whole line, till the Field-Marshal had three divisions disposable for the defence of the point attacked.

On the 6th of January, the third and fourth divisions, supported by the third Dragoon Guards and first Royal Dragoons under Major-General Fane, with General Buchan's Portuguese, attacked and drove back the French corps from the ground they had advanced to on the 3d of January; and the allied troops again resumed their old positions, each division returning to its former station. The brigades of Guards returned to St. Jean de Luz on the 8th.

On the 12th of January, the Spanish corps of General Mina was attacked and driven up into the Passes of the Pyrenees by the troops under General Harispe, from St. Jean Pied de Port.

The outposts of the left wing were guarded by Lord Aylmer's brigade from the 8th to the 11th, when they were relieved by the first brigade of Guards, and these were again relieved by the second brigade of Guards on the 14th, and so on in succession. The weather, during the whole of this period, was very wet, and the nights were cold, with occasional sharp frosts. The soldiers, whilst on the outpost duty, were employed in the construction of a large redoubt for the defence of the position, on the plateau ground just behind Barouillet, and in the formation of a strong line of entrenchments along the whole front of the position of the left wing, with batteries at proper intervals for the artillery.

This routine of duty continued till Friday the 21st of January, when the enemy withdrew all his picquets, excepting one of cavalry and infantry left in the village of Anglet, and some small posts of infantry to guard the approaches through the Bois de Bayonne. After this period, the duty at the advanced posts was done by battalions in rotation, according to seniority, with reserves stationed on the main position at Barouillet.

About this time the Duke of Angoulêmé arrived at St. Jean de Luz, accompanied by the Duke of Guiche, Counts Damas and d'Escars, and a small suite, having proceeded from England to Passages. Many of the inhabitants hastened to pay their court to the Prince, who observed, however, a degree of privacy, almost amounting to a desire not to be known. But his hopes of the reestablishment of Louis on the throne of his ancestors were manifested, by an address to the officers and soldiers of the French army, which his partisans endeavoured to distribute to them in various ways. But at this period those sanguine hopes of success were considered as premature, and could not be openly countenanced by the British Field-Marshal, who, nevertheless, deemed it expedient to show to the Duke every mark of private regard.

The Marquess of Wellington, accompanied by all his staff, was in the constant habit of attending divine-service, which was regularly performed every Sunday, in a square formed by the brigade of Guards, on the sandy beach of the beautiful bay of St. Jean de Luz. This circumstance attracted the notice of the inhabitants, who, on many occasions, were struck with admiration at the perfect order with which every custom and regulation in use in our well-disciplined army were observed. The system, however, of inflicting corporal punishment must be held as an exception; for the observance of it was always sure to excite their utmost astonishment, that such a summary punishment, among men so orderly and well disciplined, could possibly be necessary. It is not meant here to discuss the propriety of a measure, which the oldest officers, with few exceptions, assert from experience to be indispensable in the government of English soldiers, but merely to state the fact of its having operated unfavourably on the feelings and opinions of the French inhabitants, which, on all other points, were decidedly with us.

On Monday, the 24th of January, for the first time, we had a heavy fall of snow, which covered the whole of the low country. Hitherto there had been only partial showers of sleet, but now the cold became intensely severe. For several days following, the mornings were fine and frosty; but it generally rained heavily in the afternoons, which had at least the good effect of causing the snow to disappear from the low lands. During the whole of the 28th, 29th, 30th, and 31st, it blew a violent gale from the west-south-west, raining almost incessantly the whole time. On the three latter days, the first battalion of the First Guards did the outpost duty at Barouillet and, on Tuesday,: the 1st of February, was relieved by the third battalion. The succession of duty was now only for three days together, so that the two brigades at head-quarters were, comparatively little exposed to the severity of the season.

A levy en masse had been ordered in the departments of the Upper and Lower Pyrenees; and its enforcement was entrusted to General Harispe, a Basque by birth, who had the reputation among his countrymen of being alike distinguished for his humanity and his intrepidity. All attempts, however, to organize the levies, were nearly fruitless in the country of the old Cantabrians; whose descendants are a people devoted wholly and solely to the tract of land they inhabit, and who, on finding that the Allies still continued in the equitable system of respecting private property, and purchasing every article they were in want of, quietly remained in their houses; only a few instances occurring of their attempting acts of hostility, and these being promptly checked, the Allies suffered no further molestation from them[1].

With the commencement of February, the prevailing south-westerly winds veered round to the north, north-east, and east; the rains were not so frequent, and the ground dried rapidly.

On the 5th of this month, thirty-four pontoon-boats passed through St. Jean de Luz, on their way to the right wing; and from the activity observable in the departments about head-quarters, it appeared probable that the army would take the field in a short time. On the 6th, the snow on the lower range of Pyrenees began gradually to disappear. On the 7th, 8th, and 9th, the wind again got round to the west, and rain fell as before. On the tenth, it blew from the east-south-east, and brought with it the finest day that had been experienced during the whole winter. In the afternoon of this day, a hundred horses, belonging to the artillery, passed through the town towards the right wing, to assist in dragging the pontoon-boats. The 11th, 12th, and 13th, continued fine; and the roads were wonderfully improved; on, the latter day, the whole of the

1. The following extract from the Moniteur is wholly unfounded. *Depuis la permission donnée aux Basques de s'organiser en compagnies franches, et de marcher avec leurs frères, et suivant leurs anciennes habitudes, on ne trouverait pas un seul homme dans les villages, depuis 18 jusqu'à 50 ans. Les pères et les fils marchent ensemble, et s'animent les uns et les autres. La guerre qu'ils font à l'ennemi est la plus fâcheuse du monde pour lui: ils fondent sur les avant-postes à l'improviste, et sans que rien ait pu déceler leur marche, ils enlèvent les partis, ils prennent les convois. Enfin l'ennemi n'a pas un moment de repos avec eux. – Moniteur, 17 Janvier.*

snow disappeared from the lower range of the Pyrenees. On the 14th, some brigades of artillery, and a large supply of ammunition, passed through the town towards the outposts; and, for several days before, all the artificers in the brigades at head-quarters had been put in requisition, and were busily employed, under the direction of staff-officers, in preparing materials to assist in the passage of the rivers when the army should again advance. A gun-brig and several gun-boats had come to anchor in the bay; and it was rumoured, that they were destined to aid the troops in crossing the Adour near its mouth. On this day the Marquess of Wellington left St. Jean de Luz, and proceeded to the right wing of the army, to direct its movements in person; on the following morning the drums beat to arms, and the brigades of Guards, having assembled on their parades, soon after marched to the plateau-ground in the neighbourhood of Biarits. The first brigade took up its ground on the right of the great road leading to Bayonne, and occupied the *château* of Pucho. The right of this brigade communicated with the fifth division, which occupied a line along the plateau of Bassussarry to the left bank of the Nive; the left of the first brigade was on the great Bayonne road, where it communicated with Major-General Hinuber's brigade of the King's German Legion. On the left of General Hinuber's brigade, was the second brigade of Guards, which extended its line to the left, in front of Biarits as far as the sea, thus forming the extreme left of the whole army. The light battalions of the King's German Legion, with the light companies of the Guards, kept the outposts in front of the first division, and the sentries were but a short distance from Anglet, where the enemy still held his advanced piquet. Lord Aylmer's brigade, and Brigadier-General Wilson's Portuguese, (now commanded by Colonel Campbell,) occupied Bidart, and the Sixteenth Light Dragoons were in Biarits; these, formed the second line, in support of the first divisions.

Whilst the left wing was in this position, the heights of Monguerre were occupied by the fourth division, communicating on the Nive with the fifth division and resting its right on the Adour; so that when the remainder of the army should commence its advance into the interior, the enemy would still be prevented from procuring supplies for Bayonne on the left of the Adour. The Field-Marshal was thus enabled to draw away the whole of his army, excepting three divisions observing Bayonne, to enable him to carry on his operations against Marshal Soult, who, having left a strong garrison in Bayonne, under the command of the veteran General Thouvenot, assembled the remainder of his army behind the two Gaves and the Bidouze. Preparations were still going on at St. Jean de Luz for effecting the passage of the Adour below Bayonne; and the left wing remained in observation till these were completed. It was intended, as soon as the materials for this operation were ready, that the left wing, should completely invest the city and its works, as also the citadel on the right bank of the Adour.

On the 14th of February, the French outposts on the Joyeuse having been driven in by the troops under Sir Rowland Hill, the Marquess of Wellington directed a movement to turn the enemy's left at Hellette, so as to interpose between him and St. Jean Pied de Port. By this operation the corps of General Harispe was obliged to retreat towards St. Palais, and the Spanish troops of General Mina again descended from the Pyrenees, and blockaded St. Jean Pied de Port. On the 15th, Sir Rowland Hill pursued the enemy to Garris, and the Marquess of Wellington immediately directed the second division to attack the French troops, strongly posted on the heights of La Montagne. The second division gallantly drove the French from this position with the bayonet, causing them a loss of about five hundred men, of whom two hundred were made prisoners. Major-General Pringle was wounded in this affair. The Spanish corps of General Morillo was unable to advance quick enough to intercept the retreat of the corps of Harispe across the Bidouze at St. Palais, and on the 16th Sir Rowland Hill crossed that river.

On the 17th the pursuit was continued; the enemy retreated first behind the Gave de Mauleon, and the British, led on by the brave ninety-second regiment, crossed nearly at the same moment at Arriverette. The French made a show of resistance at this place, but they were soon driven in; and, in the night, retired behind the Gave d'Oleron, where they occupied a position at Sauveterre, covering the road leading to Orthes. These movements upon the right were arranged with such skill, that the Allies suffered very trifling loss, notwithstanding the nature of the country, which, from its intricacy and frequent intersection by rivers, afforded the enemy abundant means of augmenting the difficulties at every step.

When these movements were completed, the Marquess of Wellington returned to St. Jean de Luz; but, on the 21st, again proceeded to the right wing, which was now strengthened by the sixth division, under General Clinton, and the light division, under General Alten, the right of the allied centre having made a movement to support the troops under Sir Rowland Hill. The enemy's attention was thus, in a great measure, withdrawn from the neighbourhood of Bayonne; and orders were given for the left wing to cross the Adour.

The division of Spaniards, commanded by General Freyre, which had returned within the Spanish frontier, to occupy winter cantonments, now crossed the Bidassoa, and again encamped on the French territory, to be in readiness to take up the position occupied by Major-General Howard's division, as soon as the latter should have crossed the Adour.

On the arrival of the Spaniards at Bidart, Lord Aylmer's brigade, and the Portuguese under Colonel Campbell, moved to the plateau of Bassussarry, and displaced the fifth division, which crossed the Nive and took up the position of Monguerre, so as to liberate the fourth division, which immediately moved off to the right to support that part of the army, assembled under the Marquess of Wellington on the Gave d'Oleron.

Orders were received, on the evening of the 22d, for the first division to be in readiness to march at midnight. At that hour a brigade of eighteen-pounder guns, and a brigade of rocketeers, arrived from St. Jean de Luz; and, soon after, the first division filed into the great road, taking the direction of Bayonne. When within a short distance of Anglet, the whole turned off to the left by a cross-road towards the coast, observing the strictest silence, to avoid exciting the attention of the enemy, along the skirts of whose outposts the division was then marching. The night was so dark that it was impossible to discern any object beyond a few paces' distance; the cross-road along which the troops advanced was very narrow and muddy, with deep ditches at the sides. One of the eighteen-pounders, owing to the extreme obscurity, was drawn too near the edge, and by its enormous weight broke down the road-side, and sank into the deep muddy ditch, dragging the near horses after it. This occurrence delayed the march for some time, and it was not without the greatest exertions that the gun was drawn up out of the mud, and the march continued. Fortunately, however, the whole arrived before day-break on some sand-hills which border the coast, from the vicinity of Biarits to the mouth of the Adour, the space between these sand-hills and the entrenched camp of Bayonne being almost entirely covered by the large pine-wood already mentioned, called the Bois de Bayonne.

At day-break of the 23d, the two light battalions of the King's German Legion, commanded by Colonel Busch, patrolled through the wood, and dislodged the enemy's picquets, which retired from thence and from the village of Anglet within the entrenched camp. The Second Brigade of Guards, under Major-General Stopford, with Major-General Hinuber's brigade of the King's German Legion, moved down to the mouth of the Adour, accompanied by a train of pontoon boats and a troop of horse-artillery. The First Brigade of Guards, commanded by Colonel Maitland, moved forward at the same time through the Bois de Bayonne, dragging along with it the massy iron eighteen-pounders through the deep sandy road, till the whole had debouched from the wood near the Balise Orientale, a signal-staff erected on a high sand-hill nearly opposite to Boucaut. The heavy guns were with great labour brought across the soft sandy ground to the bank of the Adour, and were there placed in battery on the extreme left, fronting the right flank of the entrenched camp. Colonel Maitland placed his brigade behind some sand-hills, close to the marsh which protects the front of the camp. Whilst the first division was thus moving forward to the margin of the river, the Spanish corps advanced to the heights above Anglet, and, together with Lord Aylmer's brigade and the Portuguese, extended to the Nive. The enemy's picquets were driven within the entrenched camp along the whole front, and Bayonne was now closely blockaded from the Adour above the town, to its banks below the town. The fifth division had, in a similar manner, obliged the French picquets between the Nive and Adour to retire within the entrenched camp on that side.

For some time prior to the day on which this movement took place, the engineers and staff corps of infantry, aided by a party of sailors, had been preparing vessels for the formation of a bridge over the Adour. The vessels selected for this purpose were chiefly Spanish *chasse-marées*, which had been embargoed in the ports of Passages and Socoa. Had the wind been favourable, they were to have sailed round and entered the mouth of the Adour, on the morning of the 23d, protected by gun-boats, which it was intended should engage the gun-boats, or other vessels of the enemy, whilst the bridge-vessels should sail up the river to a point before determined upon, and there casting anchor, should be employed in forming a bridge for the passage of the left wing. As a security against fire-ships, which it was supposed the enemy might float down the river to destroy the bridge, several *chasse-marées* were laden with large booms, or masts of vessels, and with these it was intended to form a complete chain across the river, above the site of the intended bridge.

Contrary winds prevented the squadron, under Rear-Admiral Penrose, which convoyed the bridge-vessels, from arriving off the Adour at the appointed time; and without the assistance of other boats than the pontoons, it seemed almost hopeless to attempt crossing the river, as the current is extremely rapid, running, at ebb tide, about seven miles an hour. This disadvantage, however, did not prevent Colonel Delancey, and several officers of the staff, from strongly urging the propriety of making an attempt to convey a sufficient number of troops to the right bank on pontoon rafts, guided by ropes, in order to secure a footing prior to the arrival of the bridge-vessels.

Fortunately for the Allies, the enemy trusted to the width and depth of the river, and its rapid current, as being obstacles of too formidable a nature to be easily overcome;

so that, after some time, a few men, by dint of hard rowing, landed themselves on the right bank without opposition. The great bend made by the river, in its course from Bayonne to the sea, and the large wood growing on the left bank, almost close to it, screened the troops at the mouth of the river from being seen by the people of Bayonne; for had the enemy been aware of their attempt to make a passage, without the assistance of the boats from the navy, he might, with very little trouble, have guarded the right bank, and effectually have prevented a lodgement being made.

During the whole morning a brisk fire was kept up by the first division and Lord Aylmer's brigade against the entrenched camp, to occupy the enemy's attention. The French had stationed some gun-boats in the bend of the Adour, opposite to the village of Boucaut, with a view, probably, of giving greater security to their entrenched camp by a flanking fire. As soon as they discerned Colonel Maitland's brigade debouching from the Bois de Bayonne, a cannonade was commenced from their boats against it; part of the rocket brigade was immediately sent to the river's edge, and some of Colonel Congreve's rockets being discharged from thence, the boats' crews sought safety by rowing higher up the river, under cover of the citadel and works; not, however, before the soldiers had the satisfaction of seeing the rockets strike some of the gunboats, and sink them. The effect of the rockets was very remarkable, darting through the water like fiery serpents, and piercing the sides of the boats, burning, apparently, even under the water with undiminished force.

The enemy had also a corvette at anchor higher up the river, under the walls of the town; and as it was feared that a vessel of such size, well armed, might at some future day be employed for the destruction of the intended bridge of vessels, the eighteen-pounders were brought to bear on her, and continued an unremitting fire during a great part of the day, frequently using red-hot shot; but all attempts to set fire to the vessel were unattended with success. The captain of the corvette, however, with about thirty of the crew, were killed, and the tri-coloured ensign was shot away from the flag-staff, amidst loud cheers from the allied troops; but the enemy quickly displayed it again, and nailed it to the masthead. Many of the inhabitants of Bayonne came out upon the promenade skirting the river, opposite the walls of the city, to witness the cannonade; and amongst them, as it was afterwards stated, was an unlucky barber, who, inflamed with martial ardour, imprudently came within range of our guns, while, playing on the corvette, and had his head carried off by a shot which passed completely through the vessel.

The day on which the cannonading took place was so remarkably fine and the surrounding scenery so varied and enlivened by the bustle displayed both on land and water, that it seemed more like some occasion of public rejoicing, than the hazardous effort of an army to make a fresh inroad into the territory of a formidable, adversary.

The enemy's attention was in this manner kept on the alert opposite to the entrenched camp, whilst great exertions were making to ferry over the troops at the mouth of the river, on a pontoon raft which was soon constructed for that purpose; and before evening four companies of the Third regiment of Guards, the two light companies of the Coldstream and Third Guards, together with two, companies of the Sixtieth regiment, attached to Major-General Stopford's brigade, were conveyed to the right bank. The French now discovered the error they had made, in neglecting the defence of the river below the city, and towards evening sent two battalions to drive this little band of leopards, as Buonaparte was wont to call the English, into the sea. The strength of the two battalions amounted to upwards of thirteen hundred men; the troops who had been ferried over amounted to barely five hundred men. Major-General Stopford immediately prepared to receive the attack, and placed his little corps as favourably as circumstances would admit, resting its right flank on the Adour, and its left towards the sea, in an oblique direction, across the sandy point, the prolongation of which forms a bar opposite the mouth of the river. A few rocketmen were hastily sent across the river, and posted on the sand-hills to aid in repelling the enemy; and two guns of the troop of horse-artillery were so placed on the left bank of the river, as to be able to flank, by their fire, the troops coming on to attack the front of the Guards. The enemy came on a little before dusk of evening, with drums beating the pas-de-charge, and driving before him the picquets sent out by General Stopford to reconnoitre. The Guards awaited the approach of the French columns till within a short distance of their front, and then commenced a well-directed fire, the guns on the left bank began to cannonade them, and the rockets on the sand-hills were discharged with terrific effect, piercing the enemy's column, killing several men, and blazing through it with the greatest violence. The result was, the almost immediate rout of the French, who, terror-struck at the unusual appearance and the effect of the rockets, and at the immoveable firmness of the little corps, made the best of their retreat back towards the citadel, leaving a number of killed and wounded on the ground. This gallant little combat closed the events of the day.

The troops bivouacked during the night nearly on the same positions they had held during the day. Strong picquets were placed in observation of the entrenched camp, Colonel Maitland's brigade retiring for the night into the wood; where, by felling trees and kindling large fires, the soldiers endeavoured to protect themselves against the piercing cold. It was a most brilliant moonlight night, and its stillness was uninterrupted, except by the murmur of the waves of the sea breaking on the sandy beach. The contrast between the remarkable stillness of the night, and the active scene of the preceding day, was exceedingly striking. Many more troops were now conveyed across the river, to support General Stopford, in the event of his being again attacked the following morning.

The whole of the 24th was occupied in ferrying over the first division. The second brigade of Guards, the two brigades of the King's German Legion, under General Hinuber and Colonel Busch, and part of a Portuguese brigade, were conveyed to the right bank; and, in the afternoon, the first brigade of Guards was marching down to the beach to take its turn in crossing, when the squadron under Admiral Penrose was discovered in the Offing, and the vessels destined to form the bridge over the Adour making for the mouth of the river. The wind had become more favourable, but the surf increased in a proportionate degree, rolling heavy waves over the bar of sand already mentioned. This bar of sand, extending from the right bank of the river nearly across its mouth, renders the entrance to the harbour particularly dangerous whenever the wind is high; and, as it changes its position with the change of wind and tide, it requires at different seasons of the year a totally different pilotage. Towards the close of the evening the sky became overcast with heavy clouds, the wind rose, and threatened a violent storm; the whole extent of coast exhibited a tremendous and uninterrupted line of surf, and the heavy waves rolling over the bar were awfully grand. Captain O'Reilly, with a pilot, had been sent from the squadron in the early part of the day, to endeavour to effect a landing; but in attempting to reach the shore, his boat was upset, and himself thrown into the sea, having received from the boat a violent blow on his back, which stunned him; fortunately, however, he was saved; and, as soon as sufficiently recovered, he contrived to get the boat launched into the river, and was there of the greatest service in aiding the transport of troops to the right bank.

Near the mouth of the Adour, and on the left bank of it, there is usually a signal-staff, called the Balise Occidentale; and signals made from this, corresponding with others from the Balise Orientale, mark the line for vessels to steer by, in making for the mouth of the river, which, owing to the flatness of the coast at this part, is not easily discovered. The French had removed the Balise Occidentale, and the British admiral therefore sent a pilot to make a signal for the line in which the bridge-vessels were to steer. A halberd was set up, with a handkerchief fixed to it, and upon this point the *chasse-marées* boldly stood in for the river. Mr. Bloye, the master's-mate of the *Lyra*, led the passage; his boat was lost, and the whole of the crew drowned. Several others shared the same fate. Captain Elliot, of the Martial, with the surgeon of that vessel and four seamen, and two belonging to the Porcupine, were amongst those who perished. Three transport-boats, with their crews, were also lost. All eyes were turned to witness the vessels plunging through the huge waves that rolled over the bar. A Spanish *chasse-marée* had nearly struggled through the surf, when an enormous wave was seen gradually nearing the vessel; and, just before it reached it, raising its curling ridge high above the deck, with one fatal sweep bore it down to the bottom. A moment after, parts of the shattered vessel rose to the surface, and exhibited the wretched mariners clinging to its fragments; some were drifted till they actually got footing on the shore, and, as it was flood-tide, hopes were entertained of saving them, by means of ropes thrown to them;

but another tremendous wave rolling majestically on to the beach, in a moment bore them away for ever. Two vessels were stranded, but, by great exertions, almost all their crews were saved. A gun-boat also was driven on the beach.

Discouraging as these circumstances were, the remainder of the flotilla still persevered; and fortunately the surf abated a little, as the wind gradually died away towards evening. We had soon the satisfaction of seeing a long line of the *chasse-marées* pass safely in succession, and sail up the river to form the bridge, and all the boom-vessels got into the harbour. The command of the whole flotilla was under Captain O'Reilly, and under his orders Lieutenant Collins, of the Porcupine, had the management of mooring the vessels as they arrived. The boom-vessels were led by Lieutenant Douglas, and Lieutenant Cheshire commanded the gun-boats, anchoring them higher up the river than the site of the bridge, the construction of which was immediately commenced.

During the entrance of the bridge-vessels, the first brigade of Guards was effecting its passage to the right bank, about a hundred yards above the river's mouth, twelve men only passing at a time in one of the pontoon-boats; this was a tedious operation, and it was quite dark before the last men of Colonel Stuart's battalion were ferried over; the tide had now turned, and was running out at such an amazing rate, that it was not without very hard rowing that the last boat was prevented from being drifted out to sea.

The first division bivouacked, on the night of the 24th, upon the sand-hills, where the enemy's columns had been defeated by General Stopford on the former evening. On the 25th, the sun rose unobscured by a single cloud; it was a most beautiful morning, and at seven o'clock the whole first division advanced towards the citadel, the right flank resting on the Adour, and. the left extending to the great road leading from Bayonne towards Bourdeaux. The movement was made by battalions in columns of companies, the brigades at deployment distances from each other. The whole division pivoted on its right, bringing forward the left, at the same time that it gradually extended the line towards the Adour, above the citadel. The whole then closed in to the verge of a deep marshy ravine, which separates the high ground about the citadel from the surrounding country. In this manner the enemy's communication with the open country to the north of the Adour was intercepted, and the investment of the fortress and its camp completed.

During the investment of the citadel, a feint attack was kept up on the opposite side of the river, against the entrenched camp, by Lord Aylmer's brigade, the fifth division, and the Spaniards. The construction of the bridge of vessels was rapidly going forward during the whole of this day.

On the afternoon of the 26th, by the unrelaxed exertions of the artificers, the grand bridge was completed. A reference to the plan will show the situation of the bridge, and the form of the river, from Bayonne to its mouth. It will be observed that the Adour varies considerably in width in this part of its course, and that between Boucaut and the sea its stream is confined between massy stone piers. These piers were constructed by order of the French government, with a view to overcome the difficulty of entrance to the harbour caused by the bar. It was supposed that, by confining the stream between them, and giving it but a very gentle curve, the force of the current at ebb tide would be sufficient to sweep out a clear channel into the sea. Experience has shown that this theory was ill founded; for, after all the expense in building the piers of the finest masonry, the evil was only removed farther off; and, the same causes always operating, namely, the setting-in of the tide along the shores of the Bay of Biscay with the prevailing southwest winds, must always produce the same effect. It appears that the Adour formerly flowed into the sea at Cape Breton, turning to the north at Boucaut, and running parallel with the coast from thence.

The bridge of vessels, when completed, consisted of twenty-six *chasse-marées* firmly anchored at the bows and sterns, to resist the current both at ebb and flood tide; they were also lashed together both at the bows and sterns, to render the whole as little liable as possible to disconnection, from their rise and fall with the tide. Many of the vessels were moored with heavy iron guns, taken in the redoubts on the left bank of the Nive, as a substitute for anchors. The *chasse-marées* were brought up into a beautiful alignment by Lieutenant Collins at a part where the river, confined between the stone piers, is two hundred and seventy yards wide. Five strong cables were stretched by capstans across the middle of the vessels, and upon these stout oak planks were placed transversely, and strongly lashed at their ends to the two outer cables, forming a very substantial platform; which at the same time was sufficiently pliant to adapt itself to the rise and fall of the vessels with the tide. The ends of the cables, on the right bank, were fastened to some of the heaviest of the iron guns taken in the camp of the Nivelle; the ends on the left bank were wound round capstans firmly fixed by large stakes driven into the ground; and by these the tension of the platform of the bridge was increased or diminished as the rise or fall of the river required.

The bridge, thus constructed, was sufficiently strong for the passage of artillery across it. The annexed view, taken from the skirts of the Bois de Bayonne, a little way above the site of the bridge, will give an idea of its general appearance. The distance shows the commencement of a chain of sand-hills, which extend along the coast, almost without interruption, to the mouth of the Gironde.

The stone piers at the sides of the river are so broad, that artillery and carriages of all descriptions might be drawn along them. This was put in practice on the pier forming the enclosure on the right bank; for there the ground, for some extent, is as low as the surface of the river at low water; and, at flood tide, is inundated by means of an aperture left in the pier for that purpose. The formation of a road from the extremity of the bridge on the right bank, across this low piece of ground, would have required several months' labour.

A short way above the bridge Lieutenant Douglas laid down the boom-chain across the river. It was formed of a double line of booms and masts, firmly connected together at the ends by strong chains, and the whole anchored to resist the current in both directions. The management of the whole bridge was given to Major Todd, of the Royal Staff Corps of Infantry; and his indefatigable exertions in attending to its construction, and unremitting activity in keeping it in repair, deserved the highest praise. The gun-boats were anchored above, to be in readiness to engage those of the enemy, should he venture to send them down the river, to attempt the destruction of the bridge.

Chapter 7
Bayonne

The masterly manoeuvres of the Marquess of Wellington had entirely detached the army of Marshal Soult from its communication with Bayonne; and this important key to the South of France; was, as has been already stated, completely invested by Sir John Hope on the 25th of February. The completion of the grand bridge across the Adour, below Bayonne, not only afforded the requisite communication between the troops upon both banks, during the blockade of the city, but opened an uninterrupted way to the great roads on the right bank of the river; along which supplies for the army, in its movement towards the interior of France, could be much easier conveyed, than by the bad roads across the Gaves, and other tributary streams of the Adour, where every bridge of importance had been destroyed.

The triumphant advance of the Field-Marshal made it necessary to separate the main body of the Allies from the left wing; and the latter was now become an isolated corps, no longer influenced in the same degree by its relative bearing with the former, as it had hitherto been in the operations already described. It is not, therefore, intended to enter into minute details of the movements of that part of the army, which was conducted by the Marquess of Wellington in person, from the period now spoken of to the close of the war; a brief outline of its line of march, and of the battles which it gained, will suffice to keep the reader in mind of the contemporary occurrences of this brilliant campaign, which terminated only in the general peace of Europe.

On the 23d of February, Marshal Beresford, with the divisions of Generals Cole and Walker, and Colonel Vivian's brigade of Light Cavalry, attacked and drove in the right of Marshal Soult's army from its position at Hastingues on the left bank of the Gave de Pau; and on the following day, the Marquess of Wellington directed the passage of the Gave D'Oleron, by the right wing under Sir Rowland Hill, consisting of the second and light divisions, and General Le Cor's Portuguese at Villenave whilst Sir Henry Clinton, with the sixth division, crossed below Montfort. General Murillo, at the same time, blockading Navarreinss upon the extreme right. The enemy's attention was kept up during these operations by the third division under Sir Thomas Picton, menacing Sauveterre in front.

The left of the French army, being turned by the passage of the Gave D'Oleron, retreated in the night to Orthes behind the Gave de Pau, and there took up a very strong position with its left wing, commanded by General Clausel resting on the Gave; and in the town of Orthes; its centre, under Count D'Erlon, on the heights in rear, and to the right; and its right wing extended on the ridge behind the village of St. Boes, which it also occupied. General Harispe's division formed the reserve a little in rear, crossing the great roads leading towards Bourdeaux and Thoulouse.

On the 26th Marshal Beresford crossed the Pau River, and on the morning of the 27th the Marquess of Wellington directed the attack of the enemy's position. The left wing, consisting of the fourth and seventh divisions and Colonel Vivian's brigade, under Marshal Beresford, was directed against the French right wing at St. Boes. The centre, consisting of the third and sixth divisions, with Lord Edward Somerset's brigade of Light Cavalry, was directed against their centre and left, whilst Sir Rowland Hill crossed the river in front of their left, and turned the flank of their position. The greatest gallantry was displayed by all the troops in these attacks, and the enemy obstinately contested his ground, showing more than ordinary spirit in resisting the impetuous and well-combined attacks of the Allies. At length, however, the persevering efforts of the latter were crowned with success; and Marshal Soult continued his retreat upon St. Sever, retiring in perfect order by divisions in succession, and at each step contesting the ground. But the advance of Sir Rowland Hill, by a parallel line of march, threatening the enemy's rear, put an end to the orderly retreat, and the French columns, now sought safety in a rapid flight; many throwing away their arms, and all hastening to reach Sault de Navailles before the Allies, who used every effort to arrive at this important point in time to cut off their retreat. Sir Stapleton Cotton, with the Light Cavalry, pressed close on the rear of the French, who, however, effected their passage of the Luy de Bearne, a river running in front of Sault, before Sir Rowland Hill could come up with them, and at this point the pursuit closed. No estimate could be made of the enemy's loss. Six pieces of cannon were taken, and a great number of prisoners. Desertions took place to a great extent, and many of the French soldiers threw away their arms. The whole country was covered with the dead and wounded. Our numbers killed were about one hundred and eighty; and wounded one thousand two hundred.

The troops of the left wing blockading Bayonne heard distinctly the cannonade at Orthes, in the forenoon of the 27th of February; and at two o'clock in the afternoon of the same day, the division of Major-General Howard was again put in motion, to make a still closer investment of the citadel and works upon the right bank of the river. The attack commenced by Major-General Hinuber's and Colonel Busch's brigades, supported by the second brigade of Guards crossing the marsh in front, to the left of the great road from Bayonne, and moving direct upon the village of St. Etienne. The Portuguese brigade, which had accompanied the division, closed in at the same time to the ground between that village and the Adour, above Bayonne. The first brigade of Guards made a corresponding movement in advance, between the road from Bourdeaux, and the river below Bayonne; the whole line thus forming a crescent, which began to narrow its arc as the different battalions approached nearer to the citadel. The village of St. Etienne stands on high ground contiguous to the Bourdeaux road, and is within a very short distance from the citadel, whose commanding position gave the French artillery an extensive range over the surrounding country.

The enemy no sooner discovered the advance of the first division, than he opened a hot fire from the guns mounted en barbette upon the cavaliers on the two bastions upon the north side of the citadel; and his picquets began to dispute the ground from behind the garden walls surrounding the numerous villas, which are built on the summit of the hill; but the Germans successively dislodged the enemy from all these points, and rapidly gained ground towards St. Etienne. The third battalion of the first Guards, commanded by the Honourable Colonel Stuart, advanced along the great Bayonne road, and on reaching the summit of the hill in its front, moved towards the right to an elevated point of ground, when, by a preconcerted signal, notice was given to the first battalion, commanded by Colonel Askew, to advance in support of its right flank along the banks of the

Adour. The display of the colours of the third battalion, which was the signal for the advance of the first, immediately caught the enemy's attention, and a cannonade was instantly opened against them. As soon as the first battalion had crossed the marsh in its front, Colonel Maitland advanced with his brigade as far as the nature of the ground would admit, the light companies driving the enemy within the entrenchments surrounding the citadel. The German Legion met with more obstinate resistance in the village of St. Etienne, but at length succeeded in gaining possession of the whole of it, capturing a gun from the enemy as he retreated towards the citadel.

A new line was now taken up by the picquets, confining the enemy closely within his defences. The right was at the Verrerie de St. Bernard, close to the Adour, where Lord Saltoun was stationed with the light companies of the first regiment of Guards; from this point it extended in the form of a crescent through the village of St. Etienne, the left formed by the Portuguese resting on the Adour about a mile above the suburb of St. Esprit. A cross road runs along the ridge of the hill through the village of St. Etienne, and marks the line where the picquets of the first division were stationed.

When the enemy had been in this manner closely confined within his entrenchments and fortifications, preparations were immediately commenced for the siege; and, although no battering train was yet up with this part of the army, the making of gabions, fascines, and platforms for the guns, was rapidly going forward. Partial entrenchments were made for the defence of the outposts, which were extremely exposed to the fire from the citadel; and as the least display of the troops was sure to bring on a brisk cannonade from the French, much precaution was used in keeping the soldiers as well screened from the enemy's view as the situation would allow.

The left wing had but just established itself in its positions surrounding. Bayonne, when the attention of the whole corps was directed to a singular appearance, which Buonaparte, in his imitations of the Romans, would not have failed to convert into an omen of good success. It was an immense flight of large eagles, which kept hovering in the air, and continued in sight for several days. Occasionally they were seen to alight on the low sandy beach, between the Adour and the rocky coast about Biarits: at length the assembled multitudes rose high in the air, and flew off in a direct line towards Orthes. It is not improbable, that they were the same flight of birds which, for months after the battle of Vitoria, were seen constantly frequenting that scene of action, sometimes in such numbers as to make it alarming, if not dangerous, to roam singly over the field[1].

The moment that the allied army had established itself on the right bank of the Adour, the British Government, at the recommendation of the Marquess of Wellington, opened this river, and all the ports to the southward of it, to all nations not at war with any of the allied powers; and British vessels were freely admitted to trade with such of the ports of France as were occupied by the British arms. The happy consequence of this was, that the ports of the Bay of Biscay now began to swarm with shipping, for the purposes of trade with the adjoining provinces, which were daily becoming more accessible, as the Allies advanced farther into the interior of France. These vessels were in addition to the numerous transports employed in the immediate service of the army. In the beginning of the month of March, however, many of these vessels had fatal proof of the stormy and insecure nature of this dangerous coast. The gales of

1. The above fact was communicated to the Author, when at St. Jean de Luz, by an officer of the Staff Corps, who had been sent to make a survey of the field of battle ofVitoria.

wind which arose at that period were so furious that eight transports were entirely lost at Socoa and in the Bay of St. Jean de Luz, two at Passages, and two at St. Sebastian's; and ten or twelve were driven on shore.

The duty of the soldiers forming the blockade, especially those on the right bank of the Adour investing the citadel, now became extremely harassing. They were constantly employed on some fatigue service, either in cutting and carrying wood for fascines, which they afterwards made up under the direction of engineer officers; or in digging entrenchments for the defence of the line of contravallation, during the most inclement weather, and which could only be done with any degree of security during the night: in addition to which, the necessity of their being almost continually on the alert to avoid surprise, rendered their present situation one of the most arduous of the whole campaign. In fact, the troops, during the whole period that they remained in observation of the fortress of Bayonne, from its first investment to the cessation of hostilities, were never suffered to sleep undressed. The service was, besides, one of peculiar anxiety, as it was naturally supposed the enemy would not suffer a favourable moment to pass for attempting the destruction of the bridge of vessels, on which the allied army almost wholly depended for its communications.

Whenever the troops were discovered by the enemy from the citadel, they were immediately fired upon; and it was found expedient to place even the sentinels in such situations that they might be able to guard their posts without exposing their persons. It frequently occurred that they were shot whilst imprudently, or inadvertently, stepping forward from behind the walls and hedges which had concealed them. Strict orders were given not to return the fire of the enemy, as partial engagements of such a sort would be always much more disadvantageous to the blockading force, prior to the arrival of their battering train, than to the French, securely posted as they were in so strong a work as the citadel. Occasional instances occurred which showed the extreme accuracy of the French artillerymen in pointing their cannon; and afforded the most convincing proofs of the absolute necessity of keeping our sentinels in places where they could not be discovered; and where, through holes pierced for that purpose in the garden-walls, or through the hedges, they could observe the enemy's movements, without unnecessary exposure. A soldier, of the German Legion, had been posted at the angle of a large house, with directions to look round the corner from time to time, but on no account to remain exposed. Unfortunately, he placed one leg beyond the angle of the building, and in a moment afterwards it was carried off by a cannon-shot. This might have been accidental; but a second and third instance immediately following, served to convince us it was not so. A soldier of the Light Infantry belonging to those stationed at St. Bernard, under the command of Lord Saltoun, was posted behind a breast-work dug across the road which leads from the suburb of St. Etienne towards Boucaut, not far from the bank of the Adour. This road was looked down upon from the citadel, and was guarded with extreme jealousy by the enemy. The soldier was desired occasionally to look over the breast-work, but always to conceal himself again as quickly as possible: he, however, had the rashness to stand boldly upright on it, and was instantaneously killed by a cannon-ball, which literally cut him in two.

A similar instance of their accuracy in firing occurred on the 23d of February, when Colonel Maitland's brigade took shelter behind the sand-hills on the borders of the marsh in front of the entrenched camp. A drummer in the third battalion of the first Guards had got upon the summit of the sand-hill, but had not been there many moments before a cannon-shot, fired from a battery of the entrenched camp nearest to the Adour, pierced the ground directly underneath his feet, and brought down the frightened drummer headlong amongst his comrades below, who were much amused on discovering that he had not sustained the slightest injury. As it was of the utmost importance to ascertain the enemy's movements generally, and in particular to have timely notice of any attempt which he might make to destroy the bridge of vessels across the Adour, a code of signals were agreed upon, between the besiegers, and the gun-boats stationed to guard the bridge, and by which the nature of the attack might be at once known and provided against; whether it might be from the French gun-boats, rafts, or fire-vessels descending the river. In the day-time these signals were made by displaying at the mast-head certain combinations of the British and Spanish flags; during the night, by firing guns and burning blue lights. For some time, after crossing the Adour and investing Bayonne, the army was very much straitened for want of provisions. By degrees, however, the village of Boucaut, situated on the right bank of the Adour, just in rear of the line occupied by the troops investing the citadel, became a sort of emporium for provisions and refreshments brought for sale by the peasantry of the neighbouring country. Previous to this, both officers and soldiers had experienced the greatest difficulty in procuring the most trifling articles, and were obliged to content themselves with the usual rations; but when the great demand for supplies was known, and that payment was punctually made, these circumstances soon brought about a well-stocked market. The village being small, the inhabitants, in order to supply the want of houses to be used as shops, set about erecting wooden booths within the enclosure of a large field; and this spot was now resorted to by the country people, within a circuit of many miles, who brought to market abundance of poultry, eggs, butter, wild fowl, and fish, quantities of vegetables, apples, pears, and dried fruits. The prices, however, were generally exorbitant; and it was not till after a cessation of hostilities, when Bayonne opened its gates to the Allies, that the market prices fell to a reasonable standard. The sutlers, who are ever found to tread close upon the heels of an army, here also spread open their shops with stores from England. The prices, nevertheless, were kept up. This imposition, for such it really was, at a time too when the troops were several months in arrear of pay, was severely felt by them; not less so on the part of the officers, whose bills on England were drawn at a rate of exchange, so greatly to their disadvantage, that, what with this drawback, and the high price of provisions, the most trifling article invariably cost to the purchaser more than triple its value. Spanish dollars were current at the enormous price of seven shillings and three-pence each, and they were known at one time even higher than this.

The long period, during which the investment of Bayonne was continued, gave the officers ample opportunities of making observations, though not without risk, on the exterior appearance of its fortifications; and subsequently, when peace was signed, they were gratified with viewing the interior of a city, which had kept them for so long a time on the alert. The present fortifications, both of the citadel and the cities of Great and Little Bayonne, for it is so divided by the river Nive, were constructed under the direction of the celebrated Vauban. A reference to the plan will show precisely the form of the city and its defences. That part of it, situated between the left bank of the Nive and the left bank of the Adour, below the city, is called Great Bayonne. It is on this side that the great road from Spain, through St. Jean de Luz, enters the city, passing through the horn-work of St. Leon before it reaches the Porte D'Espagne; the horn-work being constructed on the most elevated ridge of ground between the two rivers. The most prominent feature of this part of Bayonne, when viewed from our positions of blockade, was the tower of the Cathedral; but, with a telescope, the whole outline of the walls could be distinctly traced, excepting near the Nive, above the city, where, from the declivity of the ground, the precise, form of the works could not be followed.

The other portion, called Little Bayonne, occupies the angle between the Nive and the Adour, above the city. It is built on a level piece of ground beneath a hill, on which stands the little village of St. Pierre, and along which the road from St. Jean Pied de Port passes. The fortifications on that side are constructed parallel with the slope of the hill, rising in the centre with its rise, so as to obviate the disadvantage of its situation below this commanding height. No very prominent building strikes the eye on that side, if we except, however, the dark quadrangular castle, situated almost close to the walls near the Adour, corresponding nearly with another quadrangular castle in Great Bayonne, about midway between the Porte D'Espagne and the Adour below. These two castles, which are called the Château Neuf and Château Vieux, are remains of the ancient fortifications of the city.

There are three bridges across the Nive for communication between Great and Little Bayonne, besides a covered one of wood, to connect the chain of fortifications. From the angle of Little Bayonne, where the Adour and Nive meet, a beautifully-constructed wooden bridge, called the Pont de St. Esprit, crosses the Adour to the Fauxbourg St.

Esprit, on its right bank. This Fauxbourg is situated at the bottom of a ravine, and is entirely screened from view on its north-west side by the lofty ridge of hill on which the citadel stands. The original design of Vauban was to have enclosed it, by a line of fortifications from the citadel, intending to continue them to a point on the Adour above, opposite that on which the defences of Little Bayonne meet the river; but this part of his plan was never carried into execution. To remedy this defect, the French had recently thrown up a strong line of entrenchments around the suburb, to prevent the Allies making a lodgement under cover of its buildings close beneath the height on which the citadel stands.

The annexed view of Bayonne, taken from a house in the village of St. Etienne, shows part of the entrenchments; above described, covering the approach to the Fauxbourg St. Esprit, which is situated in the hollow behind them. The vessels along the banks of the Adour were mounted with cannon, and securely moored under the walls of the fortress; in order to protect, by a flanking fire, the approaches to the east side of the citadel, and by their direct fire they threatened destruction to the village of St. Etienne occupied by the Allies. Part of the citadel is seen on the right. Bayonne spreads out on the opposite banks of the Adour, and appears remarkably picturesque from this point of view. The cathedral forms the most prominent object; and near the walls, on the left, part of the Château Neuf is seen. Beyond the city we perceive the celebrated Château of Marrac, indicating the point to which the ground, enclosed by the entrenched camp, extended on that side. The distance is bounded by the heights of Anglet and the Plateau of Bassussarry, and part of the Pyrenean chain shows its summits above all. Mont La Rhune and the Crown Mountain are most conspicuous; the former, seen from this side, has its summit marked by a straight line, whereas its appearance from the neighbourhood of Urogne is that of a cone; the latter is seen farther to the right, with a broken rugged summit.

The citadel of Bayonne is a truly formidable work, standing on a commanding hill, upon the right bank of the Adour, and greatly elevated above all the other defences of the city, nearly fronting the mouth of the Nive. It is almost a perfect square with strongly-built *oreillon* bastions at the four angles. A double range of barracks and magazines enclose a quadrangular space in the centre, called the Place d'armes, the sides of which are parallel with the curtains of the citadel. The north-east, north-west, and south-west bastions are surmounted by cavaliers, which appeared to be well armed with cannon, mounted en barbette. The descent from the citadel to the Adour is extremely precipitous, and there is only just room enough for a road between the foot of the height and a narrow dock-yard, along the bank of the river. Several vessels were on the stocks in a forward state, but they were left untouched from the commencement of the blockade, the enemy probably anticipating that Bayonne would ultimately share the fate of St. Sebastian's. The descents from the east and west sides of the citadel are also steep, the glacis shelving down rapidly into the ravines on both sides; but towards the north, the ridge of hill is continued, and this is the most attackable side of the work, although there are mines extending a great way in front.

The enemy erected a tall mast on the cavalier of the south-west bastion, supporting a sort of round top, boarded at the sides, for the purpose of placing there a sentinel, who was thus enabled to overlook the positions of the Allies all around. This was a subject of great jealousy to our soldiers, who were anxious to see the first cannon directed against so dangerous an overseer, whom they always designated by the name of "Jack in the Box." Many of them amused themselves in drawing rude sketches on the garden-walls and sides of the houses, with burnt sticks, apparently consoling themselves by representing Jack in his box, with outstretched arms, in the moment of expiring from a cannon-shot, which was duly depicted; their animosity was, in fact, very particularly directed against this, as they called it, unfair advantage.

Whilst the left wing was thus employed in close observation of Bayonne, and in preparation for the attack, the Marquess of Wellington was following up, by a series of successful manoeuvres, the victory he had recently gained at Orthes. The defeat which Marshal Soult experienced in that battle uncovered his depots, and the Allies had the good fortune to take possession of large stores and magazines in some of the neighbouring towns. A part of the French army retreated by Aire, and was overtaken at that town by Sir Rowland Hill, who, with the second division and the Portuguese troops, commanded by General Da Costa, attacked and drove it from its position, after a smartly-contested action. The main body of the enemy's troops, however, retreated first upon St. Sever, as if to cover the approach to Bourdeaux; and then, turning suddenly round, remounted the course of the Adour, towards Tarbes, with the intention, as it would appear, of retaining the Allies in the vicinity of the Pyrenees; a circumstance which gave occasion to a common expression employed at the time, "the French army are fond of hugging the Pyrenees." It might, however, have been done with a view to be joined by a part of Marshal Suchet's army, which retired from Catalonia the latter end of February at any rate, this manoeuvre, of the enemy laid open the direct road to Bourdeaux, and Lord Wellington immediately detached Marshal Beresford, with a portion of his forces, to Mont de Marsan, and from thence, on the 8th of March, ordered him to march upon Bourdeaux and occupy it.

This force reached that important city on the 12th of March, and was met by the municipality and an immense concourse of the population, at the outskirts of the town, all wearing the white cockade, and welcoming, with enthusiastic cheers, the allied troops, whom they called their liberators and friends. The French military, who had previously been in garrison in the city, retreated across the Garonne, but the police-guard followed the example of the people, and displayed the white cockade in their caps. The numerous forts on the banks of the Gironde, together with the ships of war, and the flotillas in that river, still, however, held out. It was not before the 27th of March, that Rear-Admiral Penrose, with his squadron, was able to enter that river. On the 3rd of April, a detachment under Captain Coode, of the Porcupine, took or destroyed a numerous flotilla of gun-brigs, schooners, and *chasse-marées*, the latter having on board several thousand stand of arms; and among them was a magnificent barge, splendidly ornamented, belonging to Napoleon, with his name on the stern, and a golden eagle on the prow. This barge the seamen humbly requested might be presented, with their duty, to the Prince Regent. By the 9th of April, the whole river was cleared, as high up as the fortress of Blaye. The *Regulus*, of seventy-four guns, three armed brigs, several gun-brigs and *chasse-marées*, were burnt; and all the batteries on both banks either captured or destroyed, by a corps of six hundred seamen and marines, which were landed, under the command of Captain Harris of the *Belle Poule*, who, in his despatch to the admiral, thus concludes his report:

> Thus, Sir, in thirty-six hours, a detachment of six hundred seamen and marines performed a fatiguing march of more than fifty miles, reduced and dismantled five forts, destroyed forty-seven pieces of cannon and seventeen mortars, and embarked without a single

accident having occurred; and the only mortification experienced by the fine body of men you did me the honour to command, was that of not having an opportunity of trying their strength with the flying enemy.

The fortress of Blaye held out till the 16th, when the admiral agreed to an armistice with General Merle; after which the Gironde was opened to all friendly shipping, from its mouth to Bourdeaux. Whilst these operations were carrying on, Soult, foiled and beaten in every encounter, issued from Tarbes a most furious proclamation, which, whilst it breathed the grossest falsehoods, strongly betrayed his apprehensions for the issue of the contest. No better proof could have been given, than the bitter terms in which it was couched, of the alarm he felt at the rapid change which was on the eve of taking place, and at the wish now openly expressed, throughout a great part of Gascony, in favour of the Bourbons. The intelligence of the presence of the Duc D'Angoulême at St. Jean de Luz had spread with rapidity over the country; frequent communications were held with his friends in the interior; the people, in many places, ventured publicly to express their sentiments in favour of the king's return; and at length the question was decided, by the spontaneous burst of feeling displayed on the entry of the Allies into Bourdeaux. Soult knew all this, and his mortified pride burst forth in an ebullition of rage against the Marquess of Wellington, who is openly accused of exciting civil war; the utter falsehood of which could not have been unknown to him. The Field-Marshal, in fact, so far from endeavouring to stir up the French to revolt, or encourage the agents of the Bourbons, declined, as we have already stated, giving countenance to the projects of the Duke of Angoulême; and he did so on principle, from the knowledge he had of a treaty being then in actual progress at Chatillon, with the ministers of Buonaparte, the object of which was to bring about a general peace, consistent with the safety of the allied sovereigns, and the tranquillity of Europe. It was perfectly well understood in the army, that an agent of Louis XVIII. was already in Bourdeaux; that the mayor and municipality had assured him the people were heartily tired of the tyranny of Buonaparte, and that they wished only for the support of a detachment of English troops, to induce them publicly to declare themselves in favour of the ancient family. It was also known that M. De-la-Roche-Jacquelin had succeeded in rousing the population of Anjou and Touraine, in favour of the exiled family; and that he also had been well received in Bourdeaux, from whence, in company with the other agent of the king, he came to St. Jean de Luz, and urged the Marquess of Wellington most strenuously to march upon Bourdeaux, where he would be received with open arms.

A single paragraph will suffice to show the state of Soult's feelings, in his address to his army: *Soldats—Le général qui commande l'armée contre laquelle nous nous battons tous les jours, a eu l'impudeur de vous provoquer et de provoquer vos compatriotes à la révolte et à la sédition. Il parle de paix, et les brandons de la discorde sont à sa suite; il parle de paix, et il excite les Français à la guerre civile. Grâces lui soient rendues de nous avoir fait connoître ses projets! Dès ce moment nos forces sont centuplées, et dès ce moment aussi il rallie lui-même aux aigles impériales ceux qui, séduits par de trompeuses apparences avoient pu croire qu' il faisoit la guerre avec loyauté.*

The events which were then passing, proved how different was the state of public opinion, at this period, in the south of France, from that which the French Marshal asserted as so favourable to the cause of Napoleon. Everywhere the inhabitants welcomed the advance of the Allies, as affording the only hope of restoring peace and prosperity to their long-harassed and exhausted country. Numerous desertions thinned the ranks of the French army; and even the arrival of a part of the veteran forces under Marshal Suchet, from Catalonia, at this period, was unable to check the victorious career of Wellington; of that Wellington whom Soult threatened to teach, "that it was not with impunity he had dared to invade the French territory, — that it was not with impunity French honour had been insulted." The almost universal sentiment, and the sentiments of the French nation itself, at this momentous crisis, tended to accomplish, perhaps, even more than the efforts of the whole allied armies, the completion of the overthrow of the imperial dynasty. The old soldiers were almost the only remaining props to the tottering government, and these, it must be allowed, fought with obstinate and persevering bravery in its cause, till the final moment of its subversion.

Chapter 8

The Battle of Toulouse

Whilst the Allied Sovereigns were daily advancing nearer to the capital of the French empire, and combating the army under the immediate command of Buonaparte in the north, the Marquess of Wellington kept up an unremitting pursuit of the corps of Marshal Soult in the south; harassing his retreat at every step. The reserves had been gradually coming up from the interior of Spain; the heavy cavalry crossed the Adour on the bridge of vessels, and proceeded to join the main forces, and to share in the honours of the field, on the French territory, as they had done on that of Spain.

On the 19th of March, the conferences at Chatillon terminated; the Allies having found all attempts to bring Napoleon to such terms as were consistent with their interest and security unavailing, resolved on prosecuting the war with increased vigour, in the confidence of being able to dictate a peace within the walls of Paris.

The memorable events of the 30th and 31st of March, which fulfilled their expectations, and gave them possession of the capital, together with the subsequent abdication of Buonaparte, are too well known to be repeated here. The recall of the Bourbon family, at this period, preserved France from the calamities of civil war. Hostilities with the armies of Russia, Prussia, and Austria, were happily terminated, and arrangements immediately set on foot for consolidating a durable and equitable peace. But the intelligence of these important events had not yet reached the south; where the allied forces still prosecuted their career with uninterrupted success.

The fortress of Bayonne, from its great strength, and the large garrison of picked troops which it contained, was much too important a point to be neglected by the Marquess of Wellington; in any other case, there could be little doubt that the allied army, under his orders, would easily have overcome every obstacle in its progress into the interior, and have shared with the armies of the north in the conquest of the capital. The siege of this fortress was, therefore, determined on; and preparations were carried on for that purpose with great rapidity, and upon so extensive a scale, that, when once the blockade should be converted into actual siege, there was every prospect of its speedy reduction. An enormous quantity of fascines and gabions had been prepared, and deposited in the ravines close behind the advanced picquets. A formidable battering train arrived at Passages from England, with an immense supply of shot and shells, which were brought in *chase-marées* from Passages to the Adour, where also several vessels, laden with gunpowder, soon after arrived. All was now bustle; parties of soldiers were continually employed in carrying the cannon, shot, and shells, from the vessels to the camp, and these in piling them up on places where the batteries were to be erected. Scaling-ladders were also constructing in the woods, about three miles to the north of the citadel.

Marshal Beresford, with two divisions of the corps which he had conducted to Bourdeaux, was recalled to support the Marquess of Wellington, in his operations against Marshal

Soult, with directions to leave the Earl of Dalhousie, with one division, in charge of that city; and to occupy, with part of his troops, the country between the Garonne and Dordogne. The earl crossed the latter river on the 4th of April, and advanced to attack a small corps of the enemy, assembled under Generals L'Huilier and Des Barreaux, which he soon put to the rout; and in this manner Bourdeaux and its vicinity were released from all apprehensions of becoming the scene of warfare.

The army, under the immediate orders of the Marquess of Wellington, had, in the mean time, continued its operations against Marshal Soult, the object of whose manoeuvres was to withdraw the Allies, if possible, from the neighbourhood of Bourdeaux; but the arrival of reserves, and the return of Marshal Beresford, enabled the British Commander to retain peaceable possession of that city by the corps under Lord Dalhousie; and, at the same time, to act offensively against the main body of the enemy. A series of movements, after the battle of Orthes, brought the enemy's forces to Tarbes, where they occupied a position on the right bank of the Adour, with the outposts in front of their left wing in the town of Tarbes, which stands in a delightful plain on the left bank of the river.

On the 20th of March, Sir Rowland Hill was directed to attack the French outposts in Tarbes, and to advance from thence against their left wing behind the Adour; whilst Sir Henry Clinton, with the sixth division, supported by Major-General Ponsonby's and Lord Edward Somerset's brigades of cavalry, under Sir Stapleton Cotton, crossed the Adour between Vic-en-Bigorre and Rabastens, and marched from thence against the enemy's right wing, with the intention of gaining his rear. Marshal Soult, foreseeing the danger of having his retreat intercepted, withdrew to stronger ground, a little in rear, and, under cover of the night, commenced a retrograde movement on Toulouse, where he arrived on the fourth day after quitting the Adour, having destroyed all the bridges as he retired.

The Marquess of Wellington lost no time in the pursuit; but owing to the heavy rains, which fell at this time, the cross roads, always bad, had now been rendered nearly impassable for the pontoon train; the allied army did not, on that account, arrive opposite Toulouse till the 27th, three days after the French; who had no sooner reached this city, than they set about fortifying every approach [to] their position with indefatigable activity.

The city of Toulouse is built on a plain, on the right bank of the Garonne, which flows along the whole of its western side, separating from it the large suburb of Saint Cyprien on its left bank. The great canal of Languedoc protects the city on its eastern and northern sides; including in its sweep the suburb of Saint Etienne on the east, and communicating with the Garonne about a mile below the walls of the city. On its south side is the suburb of Saint Michael, through which the great road from Carcassonne and Montpellier enters it. The population, including that of the suburbs, is said to amount to about fifty thousand; a number greatly inferior to that of its ancient inhabitants, who are reckoned to have been little short of a hundred thousand. From the known attachment of the Toulousians to the old regime, there was no doubt that they merely awaited a favourable opportunity to declare in behalf of the king; it was known, indeed, that a correspondence had been kept up by the loyalists, with those interested in his return for some time before.

The old walls of the city are yet standing, with round towers at intervals along their whole extent; but these defences were inadequate to secure it against the powerful engines of modern warfare: Marshal Soult, therefore, directed the Fauxbourg Saint Cyprien to be strongly entrenched, and *téte-de-ponts* to be constructed for the defence of all the bridges over the Canal du Midi, on the north and east sides of the city. Beyond the canal, on the east side, there is a long range of heights, extending in a direction nearly parallel with it; these he also caused to be entrenched with several remarkably strong redoubts and breast-works; and he further defended his position by destroying the bridges over the little river Ers, which runs in a northern direction, in front of the range of heights. The south side was the only part of the enceinte undefended by entrenchments; but it appeared that the French Marshal trusted to the width and rapidity of the Garonne, and the bad state of the roads, as a sufficient security against attack on that side, and in this he was not mistaken.

The Marquess of Wellington, on his arrival opposite the city, attempted to throw a bridge over the Garonne, a short way above it, but the sudden rise of the water rendered the warping of the boats totally impracticable. A passage was, however, effected higher up, but here another difficulty occurred; the roads were found quite impassable. He was, therefore, obliged to attempt the passage of the river below the city, and to forego a chance of preventing the junction of the main Catalonian army, under Marshal Suchet, with that of Marshal Soult. A bridge was in consequence laid across the Garonne, at a point considerably below the city; and, on the 4th of April, Marshal Beresford, with the fourth and sixth divisions, crossed to the right bank; but the waters having risen with extraordinary rapidity, it was found necessary to remove the bridge. Fortunately the enemy did not avail himself of that untoward circumstance, to attack the isolated corps of Sir William Beresford. In the course of two days the river subsided, and the pontoons were again launched, over which the Spanish corps, under General Freyre, crossed to the right bank. On the night of the 8th, Lord Wellington ordered the bridge to be removed higher up the Garonne, for readier communication with Sir Rowland Hill, who, with the second division, confined the enemy within the entrenchments of the Fauxbourg Saint Cyperien. The third and light divisions, under Sir Thomas Picton and Baron Alten, also crossed the Garonne, and took post along the front of the canal, on the north side of the city. These arrangements were not, however, completed in sufficient time for attacking the French position till the morning of the 10th.

On this day the Allies advanced early to the assault of the fortified range of heights, covering the approach to the east side of the city. Marshal Soult had drawn up the greater part of his forces on this strongly fortified position, leaving gust sufficient troops to guard the entrenchment of the Fauxbourg St. Cyprien and the banks of the canal.

The possession of a bridge over the Ers, at Croix d'Orade, which was gained on the 8th, by a brilliant attack of the Eighteenth hussars, led by Colonel Vivian, against a brigade of French cavalry, enabled the Marquess of Wellington to move the corps of Marshal Beresford and General Freyre up the left bank of that river, in front of the fortified heights, preparatory to the attack. The Spaniards were on the right, touching the road leading from Croix d'Orade to the city; the sixth division in the centre; and the fourth upon the extreme left. Sir Stapleton Cotton supported the left and centre, with Lord Edward Somerset's brigade of cavalry; and Colonel Arentschild, with the brigade of Colonel Vivian, who had been wounded at Croix d'Orade, protected the left flank; Major-General Ponsonby, with his brigade of cavalry, protected the right. The intermediate space, between the road of Croix d'Orade and the Garonne, was occupied by the light division, under General Alten, whose left communicated with the Spaniards; and by the third division, under Sir Thomas Picton, whose right rested on the river, and communicated, by the pontoon bridge, with Sir Rowland Hill on the left bank.

Sir Rowland Hill, Sir Thomas Picton, and General Alten, engaged the enemy in the entrenchments, opposite to their respective positions, whilst the grand attack was directed against the fortified heights.

The fourth and sixth divisions, led by Sir Lowry Cole and Sir Henry Clinton, attacked the right wing of the enemy, by an oblique movement, which partly turned his rear; and, with great gallantry drove him from the summit in their front, and took the redoubt upon that flank. The fourth Spanish army advanced, at the same time, against the heights above the road of Croix d'Orade; they at first got footing under the brow of the hill on which the redoubts were constructed, but the enemy moved a strong force down the road, to turn their flank, and thus compelled them to retreat with considerable loss. When they were re-formed for the attack, Marshal Beresford again moved forward, and in a short time the brave sixth division dislodged the enemy from the centre, and took two more redoubts. Major-General Pack, whose brigade led this attack, was wounded. Marshal Soult made a most formidable attempt to regain these points, directing the division of General Taupin, which had been concealed in rear of the heights, to charge the allied troops; but the intrepid gallantry displayed by the officers and soldiers of the sixth division repelled the assailants, who were driven back at the point of the bayonet. General Taupin was killed at the head of his division. Every renewed effort was in like manner defeated. The Marquess of Wellington then directed a combined attack of the British and Spaniards, against the two remaining redoubts on the heights of La Pujade, and these also were gallantly carried by the Allies.

During the battle on the heights, Sir Thomas Picton made an attempt to cross the canal in his front; but, finding the bridge over the river too strongly fortified, and the enemy, by a hot fire from a secure position behind the banks, causing his division great loss, he withdrew to his former station. Sir Rowland Hill, on the left of the Gironde, drove the enemy within the walls of the suburb, taking possession of the whole advanced line of entrenchments on that side.

After the victory had thus been gained, the enemy still guarded the bridges over the canal; and, on the following day, the Marquess of Wellington commenced a series of manoeuvres, with the intention of cutting off the retreat of the French, by the road leading towards Carcassonne; but in the succeeding night Marshal Soult withdrew his army, and the Allies entered Toulouse, on the 12th of April. It may well be imagined what were the feelings of regret, in both armies, at the great number of brave officers and soldiers who had fallen in the battle of the 10th, when, on the evening of the 12th, Colonel Cook arrived from Paris, in company with the French Colonel St. Simon, bringing intelligence of the great events which had taken place in that capital, and of the termination of the war, at a period more than sufficiently anterior to have communicated that intelligence, which would have prevented this obstinate and destructive battle.

These officers, it seemed, were only despatched from Paris on the 7th; but the delay was said to be excused, on the ground that a courier had been sent off immediately on the cessation of hostilities, but that he had been arrested in his progress to head-quarters; and thus the contending armies were left unfortunately in ignorance of the event till after the battle. There were not wanting those, however, who were disposed to think that Soult, conceiving his position impregnable, and that a favourable opportunity now offered to retrieve his military character, hazarded this last attempt, with the knowledge of what had happened in the capital. This, however, was never proved against him, as it most probably would have been had it actually been the case; and, at any rate, the information could only have been private and unofficial. The French, however, were persuaded that there had been somewhere great treachery or great neglect[1].

Colonel Cooke and Colonel St. Simon passed through Bourdeaux, and a communication from thence was made to Sir John Hope, who was blockading Bayonne; but this General did not think proper, on such unofficial information, to give notice to the Commander of the French garrison, but to wait until he should receive orders from the Marques of Wellington. He desired, however, that the officers on the outposts should communicate the intelligence he had just received to the French officers at their advanced picquets, in the hope that it might check hostilities in the interim. To this, however, no regard was paid; on the contrary, it seemed as if the absence of any formal notification had determined the enemy to take advantage of the interval, to commence more active hostilities. He was apparently aware that preparations had been going on with increased vigour on our part; and, supposing that they were in a much more forward state than was really the case, resolved on making a sortie to destroy the entrenchments and batteries. Not a single gun,

---

1. *Rien ne prouve plus évidemment, dit le gouvernement provisoire, par l'organe du journal officiel, combien se sont rendus criminels ceux qui ont osé intercepter les ordres et les dépêches du gouvernement depuis le l'er de ce mois, que l'inutile effusion du sang qui vient d'avoir lieu sous les murs de Toulouse. . . . . De quelle affliction profonde n'est-on point pénétré, quand on songe qu'un si noble sang, et de si glorieux sacrifices, n'étoient plus réclamés par la patrie, qu'ils lui ont été, au contraire, dérobés, par un Machiavélisme barbare et impardonnable! Moniteur, 18 Avril.*

however, had yet been disembarked for the siege, and but a small number of shot and shells were yet brought up to the camp, compared with the immense quantity that was intended, and would be necessary to be employed.

On the night of the 13th, two deserters came over to the outposts, and gave information that the whole of the garrison was under arms, and prepared to make a sortie early on the following morning. At the early hour of three in the morning the first division was ordered to arms, and in a few minutes afterwards the enemy commenced his movements by a feint attack upon the troops guarding the outposts in front of Anglet. The night was extremely dark, and the view of their onset was very singular from the heights near the citadel; but it was evident, from the little vigour displayed in this feint, that the enemy's chief efforts would not be made on that side. The troops around the citadel did not remain long in suspense, for parties of the French crawled up the side of the hill on which the allied picquets were stationed; and came upon them almost by surprise. Some of the sentinels being instantly put to death, two columns of the French rushed forward with loud cheers of *"En avant, En avant;"* and, by their overpowering numbers, broke through the line of picquets between St. Etìenné and St. Bernard. Another very strong column advanced direct upon the village of St. Etienne, and, in a few moments a most furious contest ensued along the greater part of the line of picquets on the right bank of the Adour.

The cross road which has been already described, marking the line of outposts through the village of St. Etienne, and along the height towards Boucaut, is worn in places to a deep hollow way; or, as the French term it, is a *chemin encaissé*, and the banks at the sides are so steep that it is no easy matter to get out of the road, excepting at long intervals, where gaps were broken down for the passage of the troops;

in many places too, it is bounded by high garden walls; and thus, when the French columns broke through the line in different places, part of the picquets were completely cut off from all communication with their supports, and retreat was impossible; in these places the soldiers fought with desperation, and heaps of the slain, both French and English, were afterwards found on the points of attack; most of them had been killed with the bayonet. It was supposed that the enemy would make his principal efforts against the bridge of vessels; and to be in readiness for the approach on that side, Lord Saltoun barricaded every entrance to the old Convent of St. Bernard; this post he had strongly entrenched, and with great ability had converted it into a respectable little fortress. The French gun-boats descended the river opposite to the limits of the entrenched camp, and opened a heavy flanking cannonade against the first division, which now moved forward to support the picquets upon the right flank of the line. Major-General Hay, whose division had crossed the Adour some time before, and encamped near Boucaut, was the General in command of the outposts for the night; and, whilst giving directions for the defence of some of the most important buildings in the village of St. Etienne, was unfortunately killed, and the enemy gained possession of nearly the whole of them.

In the early part of the attack, Sir John Hope, accompanied by all his staff, went forward to ascertain the enemy's movements against St. Etienne; and wishing to arrive there by the shortest way, entered the cross road, or lane, before described, not aware that a great part of it was in the enemy's possession, and that the picquets of the right flank had fallen back when the French columns pierced the line of outposts. He had not proceeded far, before he discovered, by a faint glimmer in the horizon, that he was upon the point of riding into the enemy's line, and immediately ordered his staff to face about and get out of the hollow road. The general, with his aide-de-camp Lieutenant Moore, and Captain Herries of the Quarter-Master General's Department, were in front, and consequently the last in retiring; however, before they could get out of the road, the French infantry came up to about twelve yards' distance, and began firing. Sir John Hope's horse received three balls and instantly fell dead, bringing him to the ground, and entangling his foot under its side. Lieutenant Moore and Captain Herries immediately dismounted to his assistance, and were in the act of attempting to raise the General and disengage his foot, when the latter officer fell severely wounded; and, as ill-luck would have it, the instant after a ball struck Lieutenant Moore and shattered his right arm. The General himself received a slight wound in the arm, and the French soldiers instantly came up and made them all prisoners. It appeared that they were only able to extricate Sir John Hope by drawing his leg out of the boot, which was afterwards found under the horse's side. As the French were conducting the General along the road towards Bayonne, he was again struck by a ball, supposed to be fired from our own picquets, which wounded him severely in the foot.

The enemy having thus far completely succeeded in his attack, lost no time in filling up the entrenchments made by the Allies on the line of outposts. They had taken many prisoners, and amongst them was the Honourable Colonel Townshend, commanding the picquets of the first brigade of Guards. Nearly seventy pieces of their artillery had been constantly firing to support their attack; shells were continually flying through the air, describing beautiful curves of light as they fell; and the flashes from the cannon were almost incessant, rendering darkness doubly obscure at any momentary pause.

In this state of the action, Major-General Howard directed Colonel Maitland to support the right flank with the first brigade of Guards; and Major-General Stopford, with the second brigade of Guards, to co-operate in recovering the ground between the right flank and St. Etienne. Major-General Stopford was soon after wounded, leaving the command of the second brigade to General Guise. As it was supposed that the enemy would push on in the direction of Boucaut, with a view to destroy the bridge of vessels, Colonel Maitland formed his brigade on the heights above the old convent of St. Bernard, to be in readiness to charge the enemy in flank, should he advance towards the bridge; but, when it was found that the attack was wholly directed against the centre of the semicircular contravallation opposite to the citadel, he advanced with the third battalion of the First Foot-Guards, under the Honourable Lieutenant-Colonel Stuart, to attack the French in the hollow road, and in the fields in its rear, of which they had gained possession.

On arriving near the French line, which, from the extreme obscurity of the night, we could still only distinguish by the firing of their musketry from behind the hedges and walls, the whole battalion was ordered to lie down on the ground, and await a signal to rush forward and charge; whilst orders were communicated to the Coldstream Guards, under Lieutenant-Colonel Woodford, to make a simultaneous attack for the recovery of the old position in the hollow road. During this interval, a hot fire was kept up by the skirmishers, and several officers and soldiers, in both brigades, were wounded. The third battalion, under Lieutenant-Colonel Stuart, was obliged to keep close to the ground, on a little eminence, which was so exposed to the fire of artillery from the citadel, that, had they stood up for a few moments, they must soon have been nearly annihilated. At length, the signal was given to charge; and the battalion, rising in mass, rushed forward with an appalling shout; the Coldstream battalion, under Lieutenant-Colonel Woodford, charging the enemy in the opposite flank at the same moment. This well-combined attack decided, immediately, the contest on this part of the line; for the French, fearing to have their retreat upon the citadel cut off; ran with all speed to scramble through the difficult hollow lane, which, in a few moments after, was again in possession of the Guards. A most destructive fire was instantly commenced by both battalions against the French, in their retreat over the glacis of the citadel within the covered way.

On the side of St. Etienne, the contest was extremely obstinate; but the enemy in vain endeavoured to take possession of a house occupied by Captain Foster of the Thirty-eighth regiment, who bravely maintained his post, although the greater part of his men were killed and wounded, till the brigade of the King's German Legion, commanded by Major-General Hinuber, retook the village, and rescued this brave officer and his intrepid little garrison. When the enemy was driven out of St. Etienne, a field-piece was brought to bear on the retreating columns, and no less than thirteen rounds of grape and canister shot were fired with effect at them, as they retreated down the great road into St. Esprit: the slaughter at this point was terrific.

Towards the close of the action, the moon had risen, and, as dawn broke over the scene of battle, we began to discern the dreadful havoc that had been made; the French and English soldiers and officers were lying on all sides, either killed or wounded; and so intermixed were they that there appeared to have been no distinct line belonging to either party.

It would be almost impossible to convey an idea of the effect produced by the numerous flashes from the cannon and the sparkling light from the musketry, or of the confused noise from the roar of cannon, the bursting of shells, and the cheers of the soldiers, intermingled with the piercing shrieks and groans of the dying and wounded. At times the darkness was in part dispelled by the bright blue light of fire-balls thrown from the citadel, to show the assailants where to direct their guns; which they effectually did, by the great brilliancy with which they burned. Some of these fire-balls and shells fell in the midst of the depot of fascines, which instantly caught fire and burnt with great fierceness; so as to require constant exertions before they could be extinguished. Several houses caught fire, and two in particular burnt for a time with great violence, casting a lurid light under the vaulted clouds of smoke which rose to the skies. It seemed as if the elements of destruction had all burst forth together over this deep ensanguined scene of two contending armies.

The loss, as may well be imagined, was severe, during so hard a conflict on a narrowly circumscribed space. It amounted, of the Allies, to nearly eight hundred men, of whom about three hundred were prisoners. The loss of the French was much more severe besides a general of brigade and a great number of officers killed, their ascertained loss in killed, wounded, and prisoners, was nine hundred and thirteen, but of these there were barely twenty prisoners. Independent of the mortification caused by the capture of their General-in-Chief, the left wing had to lament the loss of many brave officers. In the brigades of Guards, Lieutenant-Colonel Sir Henry Sullivan, and Captain Crofton of the Coldstream Regiment, were killed, and about twelve officers of the three regiments received severe wounds, and unhappily most of these proved fatal.

After the engagement was over, a momentary truce took place on the outposts, and the officers of both armies conversed together. On our expressing the deep regret we felt at the useless sacrifice that had been made of so many brave men, it was quite disgusting to observe the nonchalance affected by these gentlemen, and the light manner in which they pretended to treat it, remarking that, after all, it was nothing more than a *petite promenade militaire*. But it would be difficult to convey an idea of their astonishment, when we informed them of the events which had recently occurred in Paris, and they would not believe it possible that their idol Napoleon had abdicated the throne.

But notwithstanding they could now no longer be ignorant of the termination of the war, the French still manifested the same jealousy of the Allies, and continued occasionally firing from the citadel and works. Major-General Colville succeeded Sir John Hope in the command of the left wing, and unremitting vigilance was observed on the outposts till the cessation of hostilities.

Marshal Soult did not at first acknowledge the provisional government of France, when Colonel Saint Simon brought the intelligence to him from Paris; and the allied army was again put in march in pursuit of the French forces; but a second officer having arrived, and being sent to him by the Marquess of Wellington on the 16th, he was, at last, convinced of the total overthrow of Napoleon, and then wrote to the Marquess, expressing his adhesion to the restored government of the Bourbons. Toulouse had at once declared in favour of the King, when liberated from the overawing presence of the French army. Marshal Suchet also immediately communicated his acknowledgment of the Bourbons. Commissioners were then appointed to negotiate a convention for the cessation of hostilities, and the definition of a boundary line between the allied and French armies; and, on the 20th of April, a proclamation was issued from the head-quarters of Lord Wellington at Toulouse, containing a copy of the convention agreed upon by the two Commanders-in-Chief.

On the 27th of April, an officer brought to Bayonne official orders from Marshal Soult to General Thouvenot, containing a copy of the convention and his adhesion to the government of the Bourbons; and in the afternoon of the same day, all points were agreed upon for a cessation of hostilities between the garrison of Bayonne and the left wing of the Allies.

On the 28th of April, at mid-day, the white flag was hoisted in the citadel, and in the grand place of the town; the whole garrison was under arms, and a salute of three hundred rounds from their artillery complimented the re-appearance of the ancient standard.

CHAPTER 9

Towards the End

Although hostilities had ceased between the left wing and the garrison of Bayonne on the 27th of April, it was not until the 4th of May that the cordon of blockade was withdrawn, and that the officers of the allied troops, generally, received permission to enter the city. During this interval, a few officers only were allowed to visit Sir John Hope; and so cautious was the Commander of the French forces, that the inhabitants were restricted, in their egress and regress, to particular roads; and the French troops, as well as the allied army, were kept under the same limitations and restraints as in the time of actual warfare. But although a general permission to enter the city was withheld, many of the officers availed themselves of the opportunity of enjoying the scenery of the surrounding country, and of making those excursions, which had been denied them during the harassing and strict duty of the blockade. The peculiar features of the neighbouring districts rendered it well worthy of examination. It has been before observed, that the hilly country, between the Spanish frontier and the vicinity of Bayonne, terminates between Anglet and Biarits, and that the space, between those places and the Adour, is a sandy tract nearly covered by the Bois de Bayonne. Between this wood and the shore there is a constant succession of little hills, formed of drift sand, and of so light a quality, that it is mown about in all directions when the weather is windy. These sand-hills are peculiarly favourable to the culture of a dwarf species of vine, which produces a small acrid grape, whose juice, notwithstanding, yields a very palatable wine, known by the name ofVin d'Anglet. In order to prevent the little vineyards, planted on the southern slope of these hills, from being smothered by the quantity of drifting sands, the peasants have recourse to the practice of putting down long reeds in a succession of rows, which serve to catch the drifts, and thus to protect the vines.

The space between the sand-hills and the sea is covered by a very broad beach of sand and shingle, but chiefly of the former; and it was lamentable to observe the vast quantity of the fragments of vessels which had been stranded in this neighbourhood during the tremendous gales of the winter. Among others were the remains of two vessels that had been laden with cocoa; and immense quantities of that article were found embedded in the sand. The peasantry and the inhabitants of Bayonne assembled in great numbers to pick out the cocoa, in the search of which they were employed for several weeks.

The tract of country lying between Anglet and the Bidassoa, is alternately calcareous and argillaceous, disposed in strata of about two miles in width, the direction of the rocky beds being nearly at right angles to the line of coast. In many parts of the calcareous strata are found layers or rows of flint-stones, traversing the mass in a direction nearly horizontal. The whole tract is but scantily cultivated with grain, but the orchards about the villages appeared to be flourishing and of good growth. The greater part of the surface is covered by extensive heaths and woods; on the former; the Basque peasantry feed large flocks of sheep, which may be heard a great way off by the tinkling of their bells. The shepherd, besides his crook, generally carries a musket slung across his shoulders; others of the peasantry walk with a red-coloured stick, always with the thickest end, like a Hercules' club, to the ground and the small end is richly studded with brass nails for a handle; or covered with leather, plaited like the porcupine-quill ornaments on an American tobacco-pouch. In their features, they partly resemble the Scotch.

The country, which borders upon the Adour above Bayonne, is of totally different character. The views of the course of the river, from the eminences contiguous to it, are quite delightful, and an almost uninterrupted cultivation is visible all around. The farm-houses are comfortable and well-built dwellings, and the villages pleasantly situated in the midst of meadows and corn-fields, beautifully varied with wood. As soon as a final cessation of hostilities had taken place, permission was obtained by the Commissariat Department of the Allies, to send vessels up the river above Bayonne, with provisions for the troops. It was a matter of some surprise to the French to see square-rigged vessels venturing to steer so boldly in a river, where not even a British boat had navigated for ages before.

The Adour is a fine stream of water, and might be rendered doubly useful, to what it is at present, to the neighbouring inhabitants, by a few enterprising individuals. It is also a very beautiful river. At the Château d'Arraunce, about two miles above Bayonne, and on the right bank, the view is extremely pleasing; it there expands into a broad sweep, resembling, in some degree, the Thames at Richmond. The annexed view was taken at the time when the tide was rising.

At a short distance from Bayonne, on the north side, the fir forests commence; but in the neighbourhood of Tarnos and Ondies, two villages contiguous to the Bourdeaux road, about three or four miles from Bayonne, there are some large woods, entirely composed of cork-trees. While these trees are young, and, indeed, until they are of considerable age, the bark continues to be thin and useless; but when the tree has attained a certain age, the cork swells rapidly, and in the course of five, six, or seven years afterwards, is supposed to have acquired a proper thickness and consistency, when it is peeled of with great care, as any injury done to the thin membranous bark underneath would prevent its reproduction. The appearance of the foliage of these cork woods, at a little distance, is very similar to that of olive groves. The newly-peeled stems are of a bright sienna colour, which gradually turns darker; and, to the course of a year, becomes of a black burnt hue. Between these woods and the sea, there is a long tract of swamps and small lakes, expending towards Cape Breton, and marking the ancient course of the Adour. The lakes and swamps are separated from the sea by sand-hill, like those near Anglet; but here no attempt is made to cultivate the dwarf vine.

After the Convention, the boom-chain, which had been fixed across the Adour, above the site of the bridge of vessels, was removed; and the cables, forming the support to the planking of the bridge, were cut in the middle, and, by pulleys being attached to them, all the objects of a draw-bridge were accomplished — one of the *chasse-marées* weighing anchor and dropping astern the others, to admit the passage of vessels up to Bayonne. The cables being drawn tight again by the pulleys; the *chasse-marée* resumed its station, and the bridge was rendered as practicable as before.

In a short time numerous vessels entered the Adour, to take advantage of the temporary free navigation, and the space below the bridge of vessels became a forest of masts. Several transports, instead of going to Passages, now, in the milder weather of spring, steered at once across the bar. Major Todd, of the Staff Corps, who had charge of the bridge, found it expedient to remove the five cables, and to replace them by long spars of fir-trees, for which he found abundant materials in the Bois de Bayonne. Some of these spars were found so long, and so well adapted for the purpose that the number of bridge-vessels serving as piers was reduced to twenty-three; and, whenever a vessel was sent up the river with the tide, the centre of the bridge was opened in a few minutes, and as quickly replaced again.

Owing to the clumsiness of some French sailors, in not dropping an anchor in sufficient time, a brig drifted with the current, which was now running rapidly out, against the centre of the bridge; and; by the impetus with which it struck it, three *chasse-marées* were driven out of their proper positions, the spars and planking of the bridge all displaced, and the French vessel completely entangled by its bowsprit and shrouds in the rigging of the *chasse-marées*. The French sailors seemed to despair of being able to remedy the mischief, and were alarmed at the consequences of their carelessness; many were their exclamations, but they never once attempted to repair the damage. Not so the English sailors and staff corps, who were employed on the bridge; these, under the indefatigable activity and prompt ingenuity of Major Todd, soon carried anchors high up the river, warped off the French brig, brought up the bridge-vessels again into line, and in less than two hours restored the whole to its former perfection.

At the mouth of the Adour, we noticed a simple and very successful mode of catching salmon. The fisherman walks along the beach, following the direction of the current, and distending an oblong net by means of a long slender pole, which partly floats on the surface of the water; a slender cord is fixed to the lower angle of the net at its farthest end, and is held by the fisherman, in readiness to be pulled tight the moment a fish strikes against the net; by this simple contrivance he is enabled to take very fine salmon. He scrapes a hole in the sand, and covers up the fish to be kept fresh till the fishing-time is over, for this process is unsuccessful when the current is running strong. The market-place at Boucaut was supplied in this manner with abundance of remarkably fine salmon, which were sold at a moderate rate.

The curiosity of the Allies to see the interior of Bayonne, after being excluded for so long a time, may be well imagined; and at length, on the 4th of May, the blockade was raised, and the officers admitted into the city: The only road by which they were at first allowed to pass, was that leading from Boucaut along the banks of the river to the Fauxbourg St. Esprit, passing close underneath the walls of the citadel. It was found that this approach had been strongly entrenched, traverses being cut across the road in different places. The suburb forms a handsome square fronting the river, and from this the Pont St. Esprit leads direct across to Little Bayonne. The length of the bridge is about two hundred and eighty yards, and it is beautifully built, entirely of wood, with the centre arch so constructed as to form a draw-bridge.

On entering the city, its appearance bears a great similitude to a Spanish town; the streets being narrow, and for the most part gloomy; but in the open places, and near the ramparts, there are several large and well-built houses. The constant commercial intercourse, between this city and Spain, had made it partake nearly as much of Spanish as of French character; and at the inns a stranger is often accosted in Spanish, which they seem to think must be the language of all foreigners. In some of the streets of Great Bayonne, and on the bank of the Nive, the houses are built with piazzas; underneath the greater part of these are little shops, which supply the neighbouring peasantry with every article of dress, crockery, ironware, &c. The markets are well supplied with fish, poultry, wild fowl, vegetables, and eggs, besides abundance of orchard fruit. The great trade in hams which Bayonne carries on, is one of its sources of prosperity. These hams are cured in all the country bordering the tributary streams of the Adour; but *Jambon de Bayonne* is too well known to require further mention.

The officers were still not allowed to enter the precincts of the citadel, nor of the two castles, the Château Vieux in Great Bayonne, and the Château Neuf, in Little Bayonne. In Great Bayonne, nearly the whole of the ancient walls of the city may be traced, particularly on the south and west sides, where the modern ramparts have followed the direction of the old defences, which seem to have been everywhere flanked by semi-circular towers. The examination of these remains of antiquity could not fail to bring to recollection the importance of this fortress as a possession of England, during the latter part of the twelfth, the whole of the thirteenth, fourteenth, and half of the fifteenth centuries; at which latter period it was taken by the troops of Charles VII. of France, and has ever since formed a part of that kingdom.

Froissart gives an account of a siege which it sustained, in the time of Richard II., against the army of the King of Castile, who, with twenty thousand men, endeavoured in vain to take the city, continuing their attacks during the whole winter: he adds, "the governor of the town at the time was a right valiant knight from England, called Sir Matthew Gournay." Bayonne was the last city, in the south of France, which held out against the arms of Charles VII.; but at length, no succours arriving from England, John de Beaumont the governor, with all the garrison, were compelled to surrender prisoners of war, on the 20th of August,

1451. Mezeray remarks, that "the favour of Heaven was so benign towards the French, or the people's fancies so strong, that, upon that same Friday, they beheld a white cross in the air over Bayonne, which seemed to instruct them that God would have them to forsake the red cross of England, and take up that of France." A long account of this siege is to be found in Monstrelet's *Chronicles*, but he dates the surrender of the city on the 26th of August, and yet mentions the anecdote of the white cross having been seen on the 20th. He thus describes it:

> On Friday, the 20th of August, (a little before sunrise, the sky being bright and clear,) a white cross was seen in the heavens by the king's army, and even by the English in Bayonne, for half an hour. Those in the town, why were desirous of returning to the French, took the red crosses from their banners and pennons, saying, that since it pleased God they should become Frenchmen, they would all wear white crosses.

Besides the castles, which we found it impossible to get access to, the cathedral is the only building which seems of any importance. It is dedicated to Notre Dâme, and contains the shrine of St. Leo, the patron and protector of the city. St. Leo is said to have flourished at the commencement of the tenth century, and to have come to Bayonne for the purpose of converting its inhabitants. Having built a small chapel on the outskirts of the south side of the city, he was then admitted within the walls, and made proselytes of the citizens. Soon after he was murdered by pirates, on the bank of the Nive, and a church was built on the spot, and consecrated to his memory, in 1557. His body was conveyed to the church of Notre Dâme. The exact time when this cathedral was built seems to be uncertain; but, from the style of its Gothic ornaments, we may date it probably about the early part of the fourteenth century. The inhabitants appeared to be eager to inform us that it was the work of our ancestors *dans le temps*; but from none could we learn in whose reign, or under what governor, it was built.

We had here an instance of the extreme and ridiculous jealousy of the French. Whilst the author was sketching the annexed view of the old tower of the cathedral, from the court-yard of an hotel, in company with another officer, a French officer was observed to enter the court, and suddenly disappear. In a few minutes after, the same officer returned, with a summons for both to attend the Commandant de la Place. On arriving at his bureau, they were questioned, in an imperious tone, how they dared to *"lever les plans, dans la place même,"* without his permission? It was in vain to attempt explaining the difference between a view and a plan; and, moreover, that we did not consider the old church as a part of the fortifications. He was deaf to all remonstrance, took possession of the sketch-book, which was freely shown, as a proof of their innocent employment, and refused to return it, until a written permission had been obtained from General Thouvenot. Both officers accordingly proceeded immediately to the governor, and on arriving at his house, found, to their astonishment, that the commandant had made his exit by a different door, and outstripped them; for he was eagerly displaying the sketches, amongst which were views of almost all the positions from whence the French had lately been driven. The governor, however, with great politeness, restored the book, and offered to send one of his own aide-de-camps to accompany the author, whenever he wished to exercise his pencil within the limits of the entrenched camp; a permission of which he frequently after availed himself, and was, besides, conducted over the whole of the entrenched camp. During the time that the allied troops remained in the neighbourhood of Bayonne, the *Fête de l'Assomption* (Ascension Day) was observed with great ceremonial. The whole of the garrison was under arms. Mass was attended in the cathedral by the governor, his staff, and all the civil authorities, in full costume, and the aisles of the church were lined with troops. After the service had been performed, the whole made a grand procession through the principal streets, which were everywhere strewed with green branches, and coloured flags, and pictures of saints, hung out of the windows, which were crowded with spectators. General Thouvenot invited some of the English officers to join in the procession, and we had thus an opportunity of seeing the whole display to great advantage.

Before the end of May, the greater part of the stores and materials for the siege were re-embarked for England, and preparations were made for withdrawing the allied army from France. The Spanish and Portuguese troops marched by successive brigades, and commenced crossing the Adour, at the bridge of vessels, in their way to the Peninsula, on the 6th of June, and continued their passage of that river till the 28th of the same month; before this latter period, however, the bridge of vessels was removed, and part of the troops, returning to Spain, marched through Bayonne. Large bodies of Spaniards and Portuguese, too, who had been prisoners of war in France, besides others who had been compelled to serve in the French ranks, and were now disbanded, daily advanced towards the Spanish frontier, through the Pays des Landes. All these prisoners were miserably clothed, many were barefoot, and of a very sickly appearance. At the head of one of these groups, we remarked a Spaniard singing and accompanying himself on a miserable guitar. On entering into conversation with him, we found he had been a sergeant, and was taken prisoner at Seville; he had kept an accurate journal of every place he had been at since the day of his captivity, and showed us a long list of French towns converted into Spanish names. A lively little Portuguese soldier caught our attention, and seemed eager to tell us that he had marched in the compulsory service of Buonaparte all the way to Moscow from Lisbon; and was now on his way back again to his native capital, having performed every step on foot. A Spanish officer and his lady were trudging along with the rest; he was one of the sacred band, who had shared in the heroic defence of Zaragossa, and his wife had travelled to Nancy, to share her husband's captivity. The sick and wounded of the left wing were the first to be put on board transports in the Adour, for a conveyance from thence to England; and the British troops generally now began to look with eagerness for their return to their homes and families. A considerable portion, however, were marched. off to Bourdeaux, to be there embarked for further service in America. On the 16th of June, the first division broke up from its camp near the citadel of Bayonne, and the first brigade of Guards commenced its march on that day through the Pays des Landes, towards Bourdeaux, from whence they were to be conveyed on board ships of war, to England; and as the intermediate country has some peculiarities, a slight notice of it, as we proceed, may not be wholly out of place.

To avoid the excessive heats in the middle of the day, Colonel Maitland's brigade commenced its march before day-break, passing early in the morning through the villages of Tarnos and Ondies, already mentioned. We soon afterwards came to the extensive sandy plains, which form the great characteristic features of this country, and a very considerable portion of which are covered with thick forests of fir-trees (the *Pinus Maritima*). About midway between Bayonne and the village of St. Vincent, we had to cross a rivulet; which affords an outlet to the unabsorbed waters of a large tract of lakes and swamps; covering several thousand acres, on the eastern side of the road. This stream runs into the long line of small lakes, which mark the ancient course of the Adour, towards Cape-Breton and Vieux Boucaut. The chain of sand-hills still continues to separate these lakes from the sea-shore, leaving oily a partial opening for their outlet at Cape-Breton. After passing the little village of La Benne, the road takes almost a rectilinear direction as far as the village of St. Vincent, where we halted for the night.

At the village of St. Vincent, the road divides into two branches; that on the right leading to Dax, Mont de Marsan, &c.; that on the left directly into the Pays des Lades. We followed the latter, and in the early part of our march passed through a dense forest of firs; after which, we all at once came upon a plain, of such vast extent, and so perfectly level, that a few single trees in the distance appeared like vessels at sea, and a slight haze rendered the deception still more remarkable. It was upon this plain that the base was measured for carrying on the great trigonometrical survey of France, by Cassini, and the length of which is stated to be four thousand five hundred and thirty *toises* and four feet. Having passed along the skirts of this plain, on which not a human habitation of any description was visible, we again entered the pine forests; and it was observed, in passing along, that many of the trees were notched just above the ground, and others about four or five feet higher up. These notches were cut deep and broad at the bottom, and slanting upwards, so as to collect the turpentine exuding from the wounded surface.

We halted at the village of Castets, beautifully situated in a little valley, that was thickly overshadowed with well-grown oaks. Already we had noticed a great difference in the style of building. Many of the houses, instead of being built of stone, like those around Bayonne, were constructed on a frame-work of wood, and the interstices filled with plaster. In a few open spaces near the village, grain was growing with great luxuriance, and the spots were so completely sheltered by the woods of oak and fir, that not a blade was broken down by the heavy rains and gales in the early part of spring.

On the 18th, we again entered upon the great plains and the fir forests, the road through the latter leading in a perfectly direct line, and forming an apparently interminable avenue. The weather had now become most delightful; the mornings cool and refreshing, and the air pure and invigorating. On approaching the fir forests, the smell of turpentine was remarkably strong, and in this day's march we noticed the greater part of the trees notched in the manner before described. It appears that, in a few years, these wounds heal up, and the peasants then notch the opposite side of the tree. These forests are the principal source of profit to the inhabitants of the surrounding country.

This tract of fir forests is very thinly inhabited. The peasants generally wear long trousers, a kind of Spencer jacket, and a worsted cap stuck on the crown of the head, like a Scotchman's bonnet; their hair, thick and bushy, hanging below it. We this day saw, for the first time, some of these people striding away through the sands on remarkably high stilts, well known to be in common use throughout the whole Pays des Landes. These machines are of various heights, from two to five feet and upwards. The foot is protected by a slip of sheep-skin wrapped round the projecting piece on which it rests, and the stilt strapped to the leg. A very long balance-pole is carried cross-ways like that in the hands of a tightrope dancer, and is made use of as a prop to support them when the peasants meet and converse together, or when they rest for any length of time. They are, however, remarkably dexterous in balancing themselves upon their tall stilts, even without the assistance of a pole; and, by an almost imperceptible change of position of one stilt, in recovering their -equilibrium when they feel themselves somewhat unsteady. We were much amused by making a parcel of boys, on their stilts, scramble for ten-*sous* pieces, which they were to have, on condition of picking them up, without supporting themselves on their hands.

It was no uncommon thing to see a peasant mounted on his long stilts, resting his back against a cottage, and talking to young women on the upper floor. Many of the shepherds wear jackets entirely made of sheep-skins, and their appearance in this dress, mounted on their high stilts, is so singular, that, when seen at a distance, a stranger would hardly persuade himself that they belonged to the human species.

Our next day's march was to Laharie, a straggling village, sheltered by rich woods, which are interspersed with luxuriant fields of grain. Vines were generally trained against the sides of the houses, and it was agreed that there was an appearance of something approaching to the comfort of Swiss cottages in this village.

The post-house at Laharie is a very picturesque building, and is constructed on a wooden frame-work, with a broad gallery running along the front. Almost the whole of our officers were able to dine together in this gallery. Close to the post-house, and bordering the great road, there is a magnificent grove of acacia trees; indeed, every species of wood which we saw appeared to thrive well. Walnut-trees were planted near all the cottages and villages, growing to a large size; and the oaks were here also remarkably fine.

During this day's march we had an opportunity of observing the process of extracting pitch from the firs. A clear dry spot of ground is chosen in the centre of the woods, on which is formed a sort of kiln, raised about a couple of feet above the ground; the kiln is circular, and its sides, sloping downwards towards the centre, form a very shallow frustum of a cone; a hole is left in the centre, which communicates with a reservoir below, and thence by a narrow channel with the exterior of the kiln. The firs are barked, and cut into small pieces, about a foot in length and three inches in thickness; these bits are piled up end-ways with very great regularity upon the conical base, and the diameter of the pile is gradually diminished till the whole forms a sort of dome. The pile is then covered with a thin layer of earth, which is beaten down to form an even crust. Thus prepared; the wood is lighted from the aperture below, and it is suffered to burn till the whole of the wood is charred; the resinous matter, exuding by the heat, is of a deep glossy black colour.

On the 19th, we marched to Labouheire, where we observed the peasants cutting wheat, the earliest we had yet seen. Our brigade halted in this and the neighbouring villages the whole of the following day. The mayor of Labouheire was an Englishman, who had resided many years in the country; on our arrival, he came to entreat that we would be lenient in making requisitions from the neighbouring peasantry, who, he said, were very poor. He was surprised, though an Englishman; on finding that all the men's rations were provided for by our Commissariat Department, and that our soldiers paid for every thing else which they wanted.

On the 21st, the brigade arrived at Belin, a village skirting a rivulet, which runs towards the westward through a broad shallow valley. This rivulet marks the boundaries of Ancient Gascony and Guienne, into which latter we were now entering.

On the 22d, our brigade arrived at Gradignan, Bellevue, and the adjoining villages. In approaching these places the character of the country became totally changed —

we bade adieu to the long forests of fir-trees, and came suddenly upon a tract richly cultivated with grain, interspersed here and there with small vineyards. The houses had a greater appearance of neatness and comfort; and the dress and manners of the people bore evident marks of a higher degree of civilization, and of their being residents of a country not very distant from a large city.

On the 23d, we marched into Bourdeaux; having observed at every step the increased richness of the country, and the abundance of vineyards surrounding the villas of the merchants and citizens. The soldiers occupied a large handsome barrack near the entrance to the city on its south side, and the officers were billeted on the inhabitants.

As it would be digressing too far from the purport of a military narrative to enter into a detailed description of Bourdeaux, whose importance in the events of the campaign had been long before decided, and whose political influence in bringing about a restoration of the ancient government of France is so well known; it will be sufficient to mention, that the greatest portion of the British infantry embarked in its port to return to England, or sailed from it to join the expedition proceeding to America. The whole of the cavalry marched through the interior to the northern ports, from whence they were conveyed to England, and thus avoided the long voyage across the Bay of Biscay.

The brigades of Guards remained in Bourdeaux till the 23d of July, experiencing the greatest civilities from the inhabitants during the whole period of their stay. All were enchanted with their residence in this splendid city, and with their excursions in its beautiful and highly cultivated neighbourhood. The views from the range of heights on the right bank of the Garonne, both of the city and of the course of the river towards its junction with the Dordogne, are of the noblest character. From the neighbourhood of

Lormont in particular, the prospects are most magnificent, and ever varying, with the quantity of shipping, ascending, or gliding down the broad expanse of water at each successive tide. The plain bordering the left bank of the river resembles one continued garden, everywhere interspersed with neat villas, where the gentry of the city pass the summer and autumn in superintending the far-famed vintage of this highly favoured region.

From the heights, beyond Lormont, there is a grand view of the whole sweep of the Garonne to the point where it meets the Dordogne; and of the rich level tract on the left bank, from whence are derived the most esteemed and highly flavoured clarets; whilst the ridge of hills on the right bank, furnishes the best *vin de grave*.

At length, on the 23d of July, the Guards embarked in large boats at Bourdeaux, and descended rapidly with the current towards the mouth of the Gironde, the name which the river takes after its junction with the Dordogne. The weather was remarkably fine, and the heat in the mid-day sun almost too powerful to be agreeable; we, nevertheless, were highly gratified with the opportunity of seeing the whole course of this beautiful river, and the towns and villages on its banks. The Castle of Blaye stands picturesquely on the right bank, and its fortifications crown a rocky eminence jutting into the stream. Near the mouth of the Gironde, His Majesty's ship *Tigre*, and the *Belle Poule* and *Freya* frigates, were at anchor, ready to receive us; and accordingly our brigade embarked on board these vessels; which, on the 26th and 27th of July, made sail for England.

STATEMENT OF THE ARMY,

BY

BRIGADES AND DIVISIONS,

AT THE CLOSE OF 1813.

CAVALRY.

General Officers, Commanding Divisions.	General Officers, Commanding Brigades.	Regiments.
Lieutenant-General Sir Stapleton Cotton, K.B.	Major-General O'Loghlin .	1st Regiment Life Guards. 2d ditto ditto. Royal Horse Guards, Blue.
	Major-General the Hon. W. Ponsonby	5th Dragoon Guards. 3d Dragoons. 4th Ditto.
	Major-General Vandeleur .	12th Light Dragoons. 16th ditto ditto.
	Colonel Grant	13th ditto ditto. 14th ditto ditto.
	Major-General Victor Alten	1st Hussars, King's G. L. 18th Hussars.
	Major-General Bock . .	1st Dragoons, King's G. L. 2d ditto ditto.
	Major-General Fane . .	3d Dragoon Guards. 1st Royal Dragoons.
	Major-General Lord Edward Somerset . . .	10th Royal Hussars. 15th Hussars.
	Brigadier-General D'Urban	1st Portuguese Cavalry. 6th ditto ditto. 11th ditto ditto. 12th ditto ditto.
	Colonel Campbell . . .	4th ditto ditto

INFANTRY.

General Officers, Commanding Divisions.	General Officers, Commanding Brigades.	Regiments.
FIRST DIVISION. Lieutenant-General Sir Thomas Graham, Succeeded by Lieutenant-General Sir John Hope.	Major-General Howard .	1st Foot Guards, 1st Batt. 1st ditto ditto, 3d ditto. 1 Comp. 60th Regt. 5th Batt.
	Major-General the Hon. E. Stopford.	Coldstream Guards, 1st Batt. 3d Foot Guards, 1st ditto. 1 Comp. 60th Regt. 5th ditto.
	Colonel Halkett, afterwards Major-General Hinuber .	1st Line Batt. King's G.L. 2d ditto ditto, ditto. 5th ditto ditto, ditto.
	Colonel Halkett, afterwards Colonel Busch .	1st Light ditto, ditto. 2d ditto ditto, ditto.
	Major-General Lord Aylmer	76th Foot. 84th ditto, 2d Batt. 85th ditto.
SECOND DIVISION. Lieutenant-General Sir Rowland Hill, K.B. and Lieutenant-General The Hon. William Stewart.	Major-General Walker .	50th Foot, 1st Batt. 71st ditto, 1st ditto. 92d ditto. 1 Comp. 60th Regt. 5th Batt.
	Major-General Byng . .	3d Foot, 1st Batt. 57th Foot, 1st ditto. 31st ditto, 2d ditto. 66th ditto, 2d ditto, 1 Prov. Bt. 1 Comp. 6th Regt. 5th Batt.
	Major-General Pringle .	28th Foot, 1st Batt. 34th ditto, 2d ditto. 39th ditto, 1st ditto. 1 Comp. 60th Regt. 5th Batt.
	Colonel Ashworth . . .	6th Portug. Regt. of the Line. 18th ditto ditto. 6th Caçadores.

General Officers, Commanding Divisions.	General Officers, Commanding Brigades.	Regiments.
SECOND DIVISION *continued.*	Brigadier-Gen. Da Costa .	2d Portug. Regt. of the Line. 14th ditto ditto.
	Brigadier-Gen. Campbell .	4th ditto ditto. 10th ditto ditto. 10th Caçadores.

THIRD DIVISION. Lieutenant-General Sir Thomas Picton, K.B.	Major-General Brisbane .	45th Foot, 1st Batt. 74th ditto. 88th ditto, 1st ditto. 3 Comps. 60th Regt. 5th Batt.
	. . . .	5th Foot, 1st Batt. 83d ditto, 2d ditto. 87th ditto, 2d ditto. 94th Regiment.
	Major-General Power .	9th Portug. Regt. of the Line. 21st ditto ditto. 11th Caçadores.

FOURTH DIVISION. Lieutenant-General The Hon. Sir G. L. Cole, K.B.	Major-General Wm Anson	27th Foot, 3d Batt. 40th ditto, 1st ditto. 48th ditto, 1st ditto. 2d ditto } 2d Batt. } 2 Provis. Battalions 53d ditto } 1 Comp. 60th Regt. 5th Batt.
	Major-General Ross . .	7th Foot, 1st Batt. 20th ditto. 23d ditto, 1st Batt. 1 Company Brunswick Oels.
	Colonel Stubbs	11th Portug. Regt. of the Line. 23d ditto, ditto. 7th Caçadores.

General Officers, Commanding Divisions.	General Officers, Commanding Brigades.	Regiments.
FIFTH DIVISION.		
Major-General Oswald.	Major-General Hay	1st Foot, 3d Batt. 9th ditto, 1st ditto. 38th ditto, 1st ditto. 1 Company Brunswick Oels.
	Major-General Robinson	4th Foot, 1st Batt. 47th ditto, 2d ditto. 59th ditto, 2d ditto. 1 Company Brunswick Oels.
	Major-General Spry	3d Portug. Regt. of the Line. 15th ditto ditto. 8th Caçadores.
SIXTH DIVISION.		
Major-General The Hon. C. Colville.	Major-General Pack	42d Foot, 1st Batt. 79th ditto, 1st ditto. 91st ditto, 1st ditto. 1 Comp. 60th Regt. 5th Batt.
	Major-General Lambert	11th Foot, 1st Batt. 32d ditto, 1st Batt. 36th ditto, 1st ditto. 61st ditto, 1st ditto.
	Brigadier-General Buchan	8th Portug. Regt. of the Line. 12th ditto ditto. 9th Caçadores.
SEVENTH DIVISION.		
Lieutenant-General The Earl of Dalhousie, K.B.	Major-General Barnes	6th Foot, 1st Batt. 24th ditto, 2d ditto. 58th ditto, 2d ditto. 9 Companies, Brunswick Oels.
	Major-General Inglis	51st Foot. 68th ditto. 82d ditto, 1st Batt. Chasseurs Britanniques.
	Major-General Le Cor	7th Portug. Regt. of the Line. 19th ditto ditto. 2d Caçadores.

General Officers, Commanding Divisions.	Officers, commanding Unattached Corps.	Regiments.
LIGHT DIVISION. Major-General Cha. Baron Alten.	Major-General Kempt	43d Foot, 1st Batt. 95th ditto, 1st ditto. 95th ditto, 3d ditto.
	Major-General Skerrett	52d ditto, 1st ditto. 95th ditto, 2d ditto.
	. . . .	17th Portug. Reg. of the Line. 1st Caçadores. 3d ditto.

UNATTACHED CORPS.

Major-General Bradford	13th Portug. Regt. of the Line. 24th ditto ditto. 5th Caçadores.
Brigadier-General Wilson	1st Portug. Regt. of the Line. 16th ditto ditto. 4th Caçadores.
Colonel Vivian	7th Hussars.
Captain Mann	Royal Staff Corps.
Captain Gibson	13th Royal Veteran Battalion.
Lieutenant-Colonel Dunkin	77th Regiment.
Captain Bothe	1 Company German Vet. Batt.

ALSO FROM LEONAUR

AVAILABLE IN SOFTCOVER OR HARDCOVER WITH DUST JACKET

SEPOYS, SIEGE & STORM *by Charles John Griffiths*—The Experiences of a young officer of H.M.'s 61st Regiment at Ferozepore, Delhi ridge and at the fall of Delhi during the Indian mutiny 1857.

CAMPAIGNING IN ZULULAND *by W. E. Montague*—Experiences on campaign during the Zulu war of 1879 with the 94th Regiment.

THE STORY OF THE GUIDES *by G. J. Younghusband*—The Exploits of the Soldiers of the famous Indian Army Regiment from the northwest frontier 1847 - 1900..

ZULU: 1879 *by D.C.F. Moodie & the Leonaur Editors*—The Anglo-Zulu War of 1879 from contemporary sources: First Hand Accounts, Interviews, Dispatches, Official Documents & Newspaper Reports.

THE RECOLLECTIONS OF SKINNER OF SKINNER'S HORSE *by James Skinner*—James Skinner and his 'Yellow Boys' Irregular cavalry in the wars of India between the British, Mahratta, Rajput, Mogul, Sikh & Pindarree Forces.

TOMMY ATKINS' WAR STORIES 14 FIRST HAND ACCOUNTS—Fourteen first hand accounts from the ranks of the British Army during Queen Victoria's Empire Original & True Battle Stories Recollections of the Indian Mutiny With the 49th in the Crimea With the Guards in Egypt The Charge of the Six Hundred With Wolseley in Ashanti Alma, Inkermann and Magdala With the Gunners at Tel-el-Kebir Russian Guns and Indian Rebels Rough Work in the Crimea In the Maori Rising Facing the Zulus From Sebastopol to Lucknow Sent to Save Gordon On the March to Chitral Tommy by Rudyard Kipling

CHASSEUR OF 1914 *by Marcel Dupont*—Experiences of the twilight of the French Light Cavalry by a young officer during the early battles of the great war in Europe.

TROOP HORSE & TRENCH *by R. A. Lloyd*—The experiences of a British Lifeguardsman of the household cavalry fighting on the western front during the First World War 1914-18.

THE EAST AFRICAN MOUNTED RIFLES *by C. J. Wilson*—Experiences of the campaign in the East African bush during the First World War.

THE FIGHTING CAMELIERS *by Frank Reid*—The exploits of the Imperial Camel Corps in the desert and Palestine campaigns of the First World War.

www.ingramcontent.com/pod-product-compliance
Lightning Source LLC
LaVergne TN
LVHW090946080826
845145LV00003B/912

* 9 7 8 1 8 4 6 7 7 2 8 7 0 *